OVERCOMING ADVERSITY

OVERCOMING ADVERSITY

TIPS AND CONCEPTS FOR PREPARING YOURSELF TO MEET LIFE'S CHALLENGES

Keith J. Pomerleau

ISBN-13: 9781519625342
ISBN-10: 1519625340
Library of Congress Control Number: 2015919968
CreateSpace Independent Publishing Platform
North Charleston, South Carolina

Dedicated to Maritza, Sylvia, Michael, and Danielle

TABLE OF CONTENTS

Introduction · ix

Chapter 1 Family ·1
Chapter 2 Friends ·7
Chapter 3 Relationships · 14
Chapter 4 Mental Health ·20
Chapter 5 Physical Health · · · · · · · · · · · · · · · · · · · 33
Chapter 6 Education ·46
Chapter 7 Investing · 56
Chapter 8 Hobbies · 63
Chapter 9 Legacy · 70

Conclusion · 77
SWOT Analysis and Building Your Toolbox · · · · · · · · · · 81
          Toolbox ·83
          Don't Fear ·95
          Bad Habits to Beware Of · · · · · · · · · · · · · 103
          Effective Tools That Can Have Negative
          Consequences · 111
Tools · 117
          Self-Reflection through Writing Tool · · · · · · 117
          Goal Checklist Tool · · · · · · · · · · · · · · · · · 121
          Scheduling Tool · · · · · · · · · · · · · · · · · · · 125

Chart A: Work/School Schedule for
Returning Students · · · · · · · · · · · · · · · · · · 129
Chart B: Work/School Schedule for
Full-Time Students · · · · · · · · · · · · · · · · · · 130
Chart C: Schedule When Unemployed · · · · · 131
About the Author: · · · · · · · · · · · · · · · · · · 132

INTRODUCTION

WE ALL HOPE that our parents planned ahead to make sure we had a strong head start in life that would continue into building our futures. This includes saving money for us to go to college, allowing us to live with them until we are ready to set off on our own, and teaching us the right tools to compete and succeed in the real world. Unfortunately, we don't all come from an environment where this is the case. Some of us were raised in broken homes or had parents who themselves still hadn't figured out life or didn't have the means or skills to get us off to a great beginning.

The latter was my situation. I came from a broken home. My mother was divorced twice and was overwhelmed trying to raise three kids, and with few skills and little help. My father, who was also divorced twice, talked about his struggles of being a young dad. His philosophy was that it's best to live for today because tomorrow may never come. This caused him to be shortsighted with his money. He took every day as it came and did not prepare for his or his children's futures, figuring everything would simply work itself out in the end. My mother struggled with anxiety and depression, and my father struggled with his addictions.

I knew that I was on my own from a young age. Neither of my parents could pass on any definitive skills to me; they were so consumed with their own personal struggles that they were inattentive and did not plan for their children's futures. Things didn't look good, and I accepted that I would have a tough go of it in life.

I struggled during my late teens and early twenties. I was on my own right out of high school, and I skipped going to college because I hadn't taken the SATs. I wasn't aware of what a community college was at the time, and I didn't have a clue about how to get student loans. I battled depression and consistently isolated myself from others, and I sabotaged relationships because I didn't know how to truly connect with others. My lack of skills and self-confidence led me to believe that I would only ever be qualified for retail jobs and manual labor, where I would be doomed to work long hours for little pay. I ate what I could afford: mostly processed foods that were high in unhealthy fats, salt, sugars, and cholesterol. I couldn't climb out of my misery because I had no idea how to change my lot in life.

It so happened that one day my mother begged me to apply for a job at the local utility company that she worked for. I had just turned down a shipping clerk job that would have paid me eight dollars an hour—well below what I needed to survive as a twenty-five-year-old man. I didn't think that a reputable company would ever hire someone like me whose background consisted of jobs that no one wanted to do. Nevertheless, I applied for—and got—that job. That was the first step in opening a whole new world to me. I was exposed to the potential for prosperity and opportunity. At twenty-seven, a close friend of mine convinced me to go back to college and pursue a degree, and by my mid-thirties I had accomplished enough in my life to finally have a grasp on what it takes to build a strong future.

As I look back, so much of this information would have been useful to me as a teenager and younger adult. Amazed at what I'd learned, I began to share some of my concepts and tips with others: friends, people at work, students in my classes, family members, and just about anyone who would listen to me. Whether it was discussing the importance of continuing one's education, the way in which I was investing my money, or tips on how I successfully lost weight, people were eager to hear what I had to say. Some of those people took to my suggestions and made their own small (but significant) changes in certain aspects of their lives. A few decided to go to college, some opened 401(k)s, some started collecting coins or engaging in similar hobbies, and some were inspired to improve their physical mental/health.

While not everyone I talked to became converts, enough people did that it made me realize that I had collected a lot of valuable information that, for one reason or another, people were not getting on their own. Since we all come from various backgrounds, we accumulate our knowledge differently; we copy our role models or structure our lives based on what we learn from our parents. What gets overlooked is that we may be focusing on certain aspects of our lives rather than looking at the whole picture. Our parents may have been strong in financing, but didn't see the importance of a healthy diet. Or they may have taught us to maintain strong relationships, but thought that discovering new hobbies was a waste of time. When I graduated from college, I vowed to create a guidebook for others who may have faced similar barriers in life as those I have faced. My goal is to address these barriers and to provide tips about how you can overcome them by understanding yourself and learning the skills you may need to acquire in order to ensure an easier path to success.

To help achieve my goal, I've compiled the knowledge I've obtained through my experiences with some of the most important aspects of life. Most of the mistakes we make are the result of not knowing better: we either don't know how to handle the situations we find ourselves in, or we're too scared to make the hard choices that need to be made.

When I first created an outline for this book, I wanted to start with family. Your family members are there from the beginning of your life and are the most likely people to stay with you to the end. Family members all have different personalities and go in different directions. In chapter 1, I discuss the importance of realizing that you are your own person and that, with any luck, you and your family can love and support one another unconditionally. Family life is not always as rosy as we would hope, however; you need to be aware that when you are part of a dysfunctional family setting, *it is not your fault*; you need to prepare yourself in order to overcome what may be a rough start in life.

In chapters 2 and 3, I talk about the importance of learning how to ensure that you are surrounded by people you have common interests with. Once you understand the type of people who bring out the best in you, you should have no problem in finding a satisfying life partner. Having the right friends and spouse gives you a better chance of finding happiness; having such people around you can also give you the confidence to believe in yourself and to reach higher goals. People who hold you back will have the opposite effect: you will spend so much energy trying to maintain the relationships that you won't have the strength or drive to push for more.

Then in chapters 4 and 5, I discuss the importance of your mental and physical health. Not only are these the building blocks of a healthy and happy life, but they are also key to making good decisions and setting yourself up to take advantage of opportunities. If you don't keep your car in good working order, for example, it will break down; the same holds true with your body. If you are not mentally strong and stable, then you will have a difficult time handling the pressure that life will surely bring. While mental and physical health both sound simple, and most people brush them off, they really are the key to everything in life. And any improvement of one should positively affect the other. If you are active, you'll feel better about yourself, and if you're less stressed, you'll be less likely to indulge in harmful habits. While people who choose not to properly manage their mental and physical health can certainly still find high levels of success, for the most part, you cannot expect to attract the people you want to if you're not positive, you cannot be successful if you're not confident, and you cannot be happy if you don't feel good about yourself.

In chapter 6, I explain why it's important to educate yourself. The more you understand about your world, the easier it is to become a part of it. Knowledge truly is the key to power and success. I didn't attend college until my late twenties, and before that time I thought I was just as smart as people who had college degrees. I asked myself, "Why does having a piece of paper that tells you you're smart matter?" It matters because college develops your brain for accomplishing tasks such as solving complex problems, making connections from one subject to another, and communicating effectively with others. While you are increasing your knowledge in the subjects you are studying, the core of your knowledge will, for the most part, come from the repetition of doing the job in your chosen profession on a daily basis. College acts as a basis for learning how to learn and is a great opportunity for networking and finding an entry into your prospective field of choice. It also provides you with the opportunity to see if you will actually enjoy the field you think you would like to pursue.

Once you start finding your way, it's important to reflect on how to flesh out a successful life. In chapter 7, I review the importance of managing your money correctly. If you don't have a good grasp on your finances, you could end up in debt, with a lot of nice stuff you can't afford. Learning how to manage your money early on will help you obtain the things you want now *and* enable you to put some aside for the future. Money makes money, and the more you grow your money, the better the chance you will accumulate enough to live comfortably.

It's also important to understand that even though life has a lot of stressors (including paying bills, dealing with difficult people, and bearing with unexpected hardships), you still have to try to stay positive and keep it together while performing your job, acquiring your education, or getting your life back on track. Chapter 8 talks about the benefits of discovering new and interesting hobbies. Some people travel, some collect coins or art, and some just like to stay in bed and watch movies. Your hobbies not only reduce stress, but can also help you develop friendships, explore new interests, and sharpen your mind; they can even lead to a fulfilling career.

Finally, in chapter 9, I discuss the idea that after you go through life and reflect on your accomplishments, it's important to leave something behind. Your legacy is what you will be remembered for. If you are ever truly satisfied in life, it will be at least partly because you gave back as much as—or more than—what you were given. You can do this in many ways, including donating your time, sharing your knowledge, supporting local or global causes, or assisting in elevating the people around you.

We all come from different places in life, and we don't know where we'll be in the end. We all have our own experiences that form and shape us into the people we become. What works well for some will not work well for others. I've tried to cover as many basic situations as possible in this book to give you the opportunity to connect your experiences with mine. Still, this book may not give everyone every tool that is required for dealing with every situation that comes up, but that is not my goal. I want to help you focus more on the importance of developing your self-awareness so that you may assess who you are, what your strengths are, and how you may improve on your weaknesses. These steps, in turn, can help you develop the confidence you need to take chances, progress in a positive direction, develop skills for success, and avoid roadblocks that can lead to failure.

CHAPTER 1

FAMILY

YOU ARE NOT your mother, you are not your brother, you are not your father, and you are not your cousin. While some of your family members may be wonderful role models, you cannot judge your future by the state other members of your family are in. Through differing life experiences, individuals will develop their own individual sets of skills and attributes. Some are born with the gift of charisma, while others achieve more by trying harder. Some individuals have better memories and find it easier to recall information, while others are just plain lucky. While you share DNA with your family, you are your own person, and you need to remember that. You don't have to follow in your parents' footsteps, whether those paths have led to success or failure. Those were their choices. You have to make the choices that are best for you.

Parenting is not easy. Your parents may have had you at a young age, or perhaps at an age that they felt was too late. They may have had good parents or poor parents. They may have spent most of their efforts on their first child. Or, pour all of their energy on their youngest child to make up for mistakes they made with their older children. Your parents love you, though they may not know how to treat you or teach you. They may not have the skills themselves. They may be overinvolved in their work, relationships, hobbies, or even addictions. It is their job to prepare you for the world and to make sure that you are educated, enlightened, and goal-oriented; have healthy habits; and feel loved. Unfortunately, whether intentionally or unintentionally, not all parents can raise their children to be well-rounded adults. It is up to you to bridge the gap between the skills they gave you and the ones you need. This is the hardest thing to do. It is much easier to blame your parents than it is to forgive them and accept your situation. But only *you* can control your life; you have to accept that the past cannot be undone. The younger you are when you realize you have to control your own life, the faster you can start getting on the right track.

Be careful that you don't follow your parents' examples if they lead to unhealthy behaviors. If your parents are single and date people who only use and hurt them, you do not have to do the same. If your parents turn to drugs and alcohol because they have trouble dealing with their issues, don't follow them. Your parents do as they know or see best, but this doesn't mean that they are always right. Be careful, because we tend to repeat the examples we are shown. We rationalize that this is OK because "so-and-so did it and is fine," or that it must be what we deserve because "the same thing happened to my mother, so why should it be different for me?" If you find that you are developing these same bad habits, then you should either find a way to self-correct them, or you should seek help.

Your parents can also be overbearing. They may be afraid to let you experience things on your own or to make your own decisions. They may smother you with love, or try to plan out your whole life for you. They may not realize the harm they can cause you. Why work hard if everything is done for you? Why try if there is no penalty for failure? Why have a thought if it goes unacknowledged? In these cases, it may be best to set your own goals, become more independent, and align yourself with things that interest you. Refrain from lashing out in anger at your parents' shortcomings, because causing division will only hurt you in the long run; it stunts your growth into becoming a positive person and slows you down on your path to success. If you damage your relationship with your parents, it can be hard to get them to trust you in the future, when you really need to count on them.

Family is important. The stronger your relationships are with your family, the more time you'll spend with them. If you live far away, you may still get together for holidays and special events. Your family is there to support you during the most important times in your life; even if you are having trouble dealing with certain members of your family, make peace with them and love them.

If you are unhappy with the direction a family member has taken, then the best thing you can do is to set a positive example for that person. If you have a competitive family, convince a sibling to go back to school with you and to compete to see who can get a higher GPA or graduate first. Keep in mind, though, that if competition has a negative effect, then it may not be a helpful tool. If a sibling is having trouble losing weight, encourage him or her to participate in outside activities or to learn how to cook new, healthier recipes that don't sacrifice taste.

You should also take every opportunity to learn things from others in your family. Different people have different skills and knowledge. Some are good with their hands, others have artistic or musical abilities, and some may be good at math or problem solving. The more tools you can fit into your life, the more opportunities you'll have down the road. If you have bright and talented people in your family, don't be afraid to learn from their experiences and feed off their vast knowledge.

Sometimes you'll have to do things for your family that you may not want to do, such as helping them move, lending them money, or taking them to the hospital or airport. Remember that they also do things for you that they may not enjoy. If you fail to be there for them when they need you, be prepared for the same reaction when you need help.

I am in no way saying to let your family take advantage of you. If a relative keeps borrowing money with no clear intention of paying you back, then that is an issue that needs to be examined carefully. There can be different reasons for their actions. They could be going through hard times, or feeding an addiction they cannot control—or they may simply realize that they can get away with it. You know your family; you have known them your whole life. Don't be blind to the fact that they may be taking advantage of you, but do consider that they may need your help. It's easy to get angry or resent them. Again, though, you are not them, and they are not you: even though you were raised in the same

3

household, you will have different personalities and will have encountered different experiences that make you who you are.

If you felt neglected or put down all the time when you were young, you may feel the need to always be the best at what you do in order to stand out and to get that feeling of gratification you never received as a child. This could lead to being independent and creative, and always trying to find ways to better the situation. People like this take charge and learn to be compassionate because they know what it feels like to be on the wrong side of someone's favor. Alternately, you may feel worthless and unloved, and you give up any time there is a conflict. You may simply march through the bad times, think nothing of how you're treated, and carry on with your life. You may become angry and build up large amounts of anger and resentment, such that you lash out against anyone who tries to get close to you.

What is it that triggers the direction you take? Some of it is your personality; you may be easygoing and able to let things go. You may be a "deep" person who can rationalize the actions of the people in your life. You may be selfish and magnify every slight that is dealt to you. You may be shy and close down when you should open up. You may be emotional and have trouble rationalizing others' behavior, and you blame yourself for your treatment. And so on. The same thing can be said for children who had an easy path in life. While children with well-to-do parents have access to more resources, which can lead to a higher chance of success, this is not always the case. Some kids who are spoiled and whose parents planned everything out for them can become lazy and develop the impression that everything should come easily. They never learn how to deal with difficult situations because they are sheltered from them. Instead of dealing with the situations and looking for resolutions, they may blame others and find other mechanisms to cope, such as overeating or drug use.

Children with an easy path could also become charismatic and confident that things will work out. They may become proficient networkers and have little trouble in finding the right people who can offer solutions to their problems. Many of us often look to such people because we sense strength and calm in them.

If you can analyze why you or family members act the way they do and try to figure out what events in their lives shaped them, then you may be able to find peace and unity with them. If you would like to help family members because you have the means, you can do so in a way that won't cause them to become dependent on or enabled by you. If they are struggling and cannot afford their bills, then help them by buying them food or putting a utility bill in your name and paying for it. If they have an addiction, do not abet it. Do not share medications or money, even if you have the ability to do so. If you support their addiction, then you have no right to be angry when they continue to spiral down into misery. You should encourage them to get back on their feet, live healthier life-styles, and believe in themselves.

Sometimes you lose touch with family members as you get older. It could be because you moved, you have too much going on, or you have come to the realization that you have nothing in common. Whatever the case, it's still important to try to keep an ongoing, positive relationship with your family members, no matter how hard it may be. Friends will come and go, but family is forever. Just because you feel that you are not like other members of your family doesn't mean that you don't have a strong role to play. They can sometimes drive you insane, but you can control how much or how little interaction you have with them. If you give up on them completely, they may fall deeper into their ailments and have less confidence in themselves. You have to be the lightning rod of change, and you have to be a good example for others. If you cannot offer forgiveness and kindness to your own kin, then what right do you have to expect the same from others?

While you should try your best with family members, don't let them bring you down. There may come a time when you have tried your best and keep getting the same result, and you will then realize that there is nothing else you can do. You can't let a family member drive you to bankruptcy, depression, or addiction. It is all too easy to be influenced or conned by the people you love the most. Try your best, but do not allow yourself to be pulled down, taken for granted, or used.

But most of all, remember that you can be that positive influence on others. People who have faith inspire others to make positive changes in themselves. Sometimes they'll make mistakes and do things that hurt you. You should realize that this backlash may be coming from a sense of fear, jealousy, or frustration. Don't allow this to discourage you. Sometimes your hard work will be rewarded, but other times it won't. You have to realize that your family may include characters who do not fit your view of a perfect family. You must learn how to deal with them, or you must accept that you may not be able to change them. If they are having an especially negative effect on your life, you may come to the realization that it's best to simply let them go.

CHAPTER 2

FRIENDS

SURROUND YOURSELF WITH people who complement you. While having similar interests as others will not guarantee successful friendships, it does increase your chances. You should try to align yourself with people who share similar visions and values with you. The strongest friendships are with those who not only help you when you are low, but those who also keep you soaring when you're high. Success matters to people, and those who are not as ambitious or studious as you may begin to feel jealousy or regret over your accomplishments. People fail in life for many reasons, mainly because they give up too quickly instead of fighting for more. You need people who love and trust you, but, as you grow, people will start to have different interests and priorities. The more you align yourself with people who make you a better person, the more likely they will be to stay in your life and grow with you instead of away from you.

One of the hardest things to do in life is to realize that a friendship has ended. You have so many fond memories of the people you were with at certain times of your life that it makes it hard to let them go. Clinging to the past is one of the unhealthiest things you can do. You had that moment, and now it is time to build new and better moments. If someone no longer gives you the same effort in the friendship, or you have to give far more than you get back, then it is time to let go. Life is hard enough without the people you trust the most holding you back. Bad friends take you out drinking when they know you should be studying; they offer you a cigarette when you're trying to quit because they don't want to lose that connection with you; or they convince you to go out and spend money when they know your rent is due. It isn't because they don't care about you; it's because misery loves company. The further you move away from the things they are doing, the more they will realize that they are losing you. Good friends will try to improve their lives in order to grow with you; they will try to get better jobs, become more educated, quit bad habits, or join you in picking up new sports or hobbies.

If you wake up and don't like your situation, and you feel like you aren't attracting the right kind of people, then assess the type of people you have attracted and retained, see what they have in common, and decide if they are helping you or harming you. A girl-chasing party king may be the best friend to have when you are twenty, but as you settle down in your thirties and start a family, your values may change; if that friend is still chasing women and spending weekends at the bars, then you may no longer have much in common.

Friends also influence you more than you know. These are the people whom you learn from, trust the most, and go through a variety of experiences with. You play sports together or build forts from a young age, and you rush out into the world together. Becoming accepted into a group can really affect you, however, depending on the kind of group it is. Groups may be divided into three varieties: positive groups, negative groups, and temporary groups.

Being a part of a positive group is the pinnacle of life. This group is usually tight-knit and understanding, and the people stay close throughout your life. You learn and grow together, and are there for one another when things get tough. In these groups, you are appreciated for your uniqueness and the special qualities you bring to the group. The strength of these groups is that they have enough trust and security to overcome problems or situations that might end more fragile relationships. Members of such groups work through their problems and pick one another up when necessary. They are supportive and they give good advice, and they don't abandon you when things get hard. They share common goals and positive aspirations. The people in this group can do well in life because they are secure and approachable and they know how to network. They believe every individual brings unique qualities to bear, and they can see the value in people who might otherwise be overlooked.

Having a great support system should never be overlooked: you need people you can depend on throughout your life. The more positive people you surround yourself with, the better decisions you'll make, and the better influences you'll have to make sure you stay on the right track.

Negative groups can also be tight-knit and supportive, and they can also remain close throughout your life. Unfortunately, they may have the opposite effect of a positive group: they can support your negative habits, and they can make it feel acceptable for you to fail and then to blame it on others. As the saying goes, "misery loves company," and those who are down often find it easier to blame others rather than taking accountability for their actions. If the people you surround yourself with are in a similar negative situation and, instead of helping you get out of the rut you find yourself in, support you in staying there, then it is clear what is going on. A good way to explain this situation is to take two alcoholic friends. One is having health problems and decides to quit drinking as a result, but the other has no intention of doing the same. Instead of helping the first one quit and thus improve both of their situations, the second friend may be tempted to convince the one who is experiencing health problems to have just one more drink. People like this are valuing their personal desires and selfish needs over those of their friends. The negative influence of this friendship makes it unlikely that the friend with health problems will quit drinking, and will risk further damage as a result. When it is a lifelong friend whom you love and trust, it is hard to say no and turn away. The need for companionship can override the need to make the correct decisions you need to make.

A positive group would handle this situation differently. People in this group would work together to make sure the friend not only quit drinking, but also that he was learning about potential risks, eating healthier, and exercising. Friendship, like any good relationship, means putting someone else's needs ahead of your own so that you can continue a positive relationship for as long as possible. Putting someone's needs ahead of your own shows how much you care about your friend and how committed you are to the relationship. Cherish these types of people, because they make a strong foundation for your life.

Negative groups can lower your self-esteem. They don't work as hard to achieve success for themselves, and, by associating with this group, you may become comfortable with accomplishing less. When you feel negative, it's hard to see anything positive on the horizon; even when you do make an effort, you can become discouraged easily and return to your previous situation. You can be influenced to abuse substances or commit actions you know are wrong just to fit in and be a part of the group, like stealing or fighting. The more indifferent you become to taking part in bad behavior, the more you become desensitized to it, and the harder it becomes to realize that you can be more than what you are. It's a vicious cycle. It's like gaining weight—you start to feel bad about yourself, so you eat more, and you gain more weight. Suddenly, your weight is out of control, and you feel like there is little you can do... so you eat more and you gain even more weight. This can lead to health problems and issues with self-esteem, and could lead to the deterioration of relationships and the loss of possible careers and ambition. The further you go down a negative path, the more difficult—but not impossible—it becomes to turn around and head for the positive path.

Temporary groups are short-term friendships that might include friends from school or work, friends of friends, friends of your girlfriend or boyfriend, or people whom you randomly meet and soon part ways with. These relationships generally don't last, because when the connection that brought you together is severed, the relationship usually ends. For example, it is difficult to be friends with someone whom you just broke up with. It could make the situation awkward for any friends you have in common by creating a position where they may be forced to choose you over your ex. Some of the people you meet in this fashion, however, may become long-term friends (either positive or negative); sometimes you simply lose touch from being busy or having closer friends who take up your time.

Temporary groups are good because they help you see how other people interact; they can give you a different perspective on life. Each "clique" of friends is drawn together by unique characteristics. One group may love sports, beaches, and drinking beer; one may fancy poetry, traveling, and playing music; while another may be composed of jokesters and movie buffs. As a member of such a group, you may pick up different hobbies or mannerisms or learn how to interact with people who come from different places or walks of life. The relationships formed from temporary groups are generally the best: even though they are short, they are usually filled with self-discovery and they allow you to learn about others' experiences. You can let your guard down and become a part of the adventure. You can get swept up and lost in these groups, though, so you have to be careful. Since you are not really familiar with the members of this group, you might find yourself in a situation where you are alone and uncomfortable. These relationships spring up fast, and it may be hard for you to get a reading on the people you are surrounded with, or for them to do the same with you. You may quickly find that your philosophies conflict with those of the other members, and you'll be left feeling vulnerable. Be aware of the situations you get into and make sure you have a safe escape lined up when you are associating with new people you don't know much about.

You also don't want to depend entirely on short-term relationships, because such dependency can set negative precedents. First, it can become hard for you to ever trust that a relationship will last: you constantly move from one group to another and never truly build a foundation of trust or loyalty. You never know who will be there for you no matter what, or who is a "fair-weather" friend. Will that person be there for you if you need help moving, or are stuck somewhere and need a ride? Can you call that person to talk to when things are bad? This can carry on long into your life, until you feel that no one around you will be there for long; when this happens, you will have trouble developing strong, lasting relationships.

Second, you may convince yourself that change is inevitable. You may get yourself into the mind-set of, "I have learned all I can from this person; it's time to move on," or "I'm bored with this person; what else is out there?" When you're always looking for the next best thing, you may move on too quickly from the right people and not allow them to reveal who they truly are. They may be shy and not open up as quickly, or they may never have a chance to prove how special they are. It is one thing to know someone isn't right for you; it's another to take advantage of the situation because you can. If you can't treat people with the kindness they deserve, why would they do the same for you?

Finally, short-term relationships can be taxing. When you meet so many people, it's hard to even remember everyone's names, and it may be difficult to know which relationships show potential. This can be fun, but it limits your ability to grow and should be avoided. It's wise to network, but you really need to set roots and find people to grow with. From doing this, you can begin to shape your life and recognize the type of people you want in it. You may grow insecure and become too dependent on people, and, in turn, you could become the proverbial albatross that people avoid. Alternately, they may see you as someone who doesn't invest time in others. Relationship-building is an important skill in life, and you should invest a good amount of yourself in developing it.

While it's important to build relationships, you should not let failed relationships define you. Some people are either incompatible, they're not in the same place in life, or they don't share similar visions. Losing someone should not be the end of you. Take some time to reflect about what went right and what went wrong, and learn from it. Look at the situation as an opportunity to find people who are a better fit for where you are in life right now and who can help you get to where you want to go.

Never belittle yourself or chase people who are gone. When you allow yourself to feel that desperate, then you will either get used by these people, or you will continue to hurt your morale, put yourself in bad situations, miss out on the people who want to be with you, or cause the people who are in your life to feel like they can no longer relate to you. It's difficult to win friends when you appear clingy, overly needy, or desperate to find someone like you; people will wonder what is wrong with you. How can they build their foundation with you when you don't demonstrate a foundation yourself? As you search for people who will complement you and will help you grow, others are looking for the same thing from you in return.

If you are guilty of being this type of person, you should take a step back and work on yourself. Figure out what you're looking for in others, and do a strength-and-weakness evaluation. Start by listing some of the reasons why some of your relationships did *not* work out, then examine why some of your current relationships *are* working. Finally, try to determine what you need to improve on internally in order to get yourself to a point where you will feel steady and secure being alone. Then you can begin to search for people who fit your criteria.

When people see that you have your act together, it will attract them to you. Don't get overanxious and revert to your prior behaviors, or you'll end up with the same negative results you've had earlier. If you can't figure out these things on your own, then ask some close friends or family members to help you break yourself down in an honest and constructive way. If you don't have anyone who can help you, it may be worthwhile to explore getting professional help.

The inability to change your behaviors can make it hard to improve your situation. Sometimes we don't have the strength to overcome things on our own, but we must learn that we are worth something, and that we won't allow people to take advantage of us. Building relationships with people who share our vision is vitally important. Of course you want to build these relationships with positive groups and not negative groups, but friends who last a lifetime are great friends to have. Try your best to keep moving forward and to help one another accomplish your own individual hopes and dreams.

CHAPTER 3

RELATIONSHIPS

USE THE SAME tools to find a life partner as you do when creating and making friendships: you want someone who complements you, challenges you to grow, and has common values and visions for the future. Your partner should be the ultimate best friend: the one you know you can count on above all others. You can't go into a relationship thinking that everything will always go right, however, because maintaining a healthy relationship is work. Even when you take two people who are trying to attain what they feel is the perfect scenario, it is unlikely that they will agree about everything. You have to be able to fight for the things that are most important, but be willing to compromise on those that are less so. Even if a number of things are important to you, you may still need to compromise so that both of you feel like you are getting at least part of what you wanted. The better you are at compromise, the more harmonious your relationship will be. A strong relationship can lead to a better life because you will have that one person whom you know you can trust and count on in difficult times, and your partner will feel the same.

You also have to be ready to let go if it isn't working. Trying to keep a failed relationship together when nothing appears to be getting better is unhealthy. You may both be terrific people, but not when you are together. If you find yourselves *constantly* disagreeing and arguing over silly things, that may be a sign that you are both looking for different things. (Maybe not better things: just different things.) By staying together, you are doing both of you a disservice by preventing yourselves from finding better partners. It could be that you are too much alike, or that you have too many differences. All things require balance. If you don't have balance in your relationship, then it will be hard for either partner to be truly happy. If you feel that your disagreements are minor, then you could try counseling or you could ask a friend or family member whom you trust to mediate your grievances. This will let you be open and honest and allow you to get feedback from a third-party source. It might help you to see things differently and may open a new line of dialogue that could help to steer the relationship back on course.

If you want to be sure that someone loves you, you only need to be mindful on how they are treating you. In using the example of a boy meeting a new girl, he shouldn't have to wonder if she's interested in him. If he's on her mind, then she will go out of her way to spend time with him. If she doesn't, there's a good reason for it: she may be involved in maintaining other relationships, or she may not be interested in getting serious. Alternately, she may simply be shy, and need some time before she feels ready to open up.

People who are deeply in love, however, tend to feel anxious when they are separated, even during difficult times. Even successful relationships require a lot of work to maintain and keep them healthy. If you feel like you are working harder than your partner is at maintaining the relationship, then it may be time to talk about it. You have to set goals and/or limits to what you each want or are unwilling to accept. If you find that even after this point there is no change, then it could be time to move on. Be honest with yourself and stand by your decisions; your relationship with your partner is the most important one in your life. This is the person whom you trust and love the most. If you have exerted all of your options (such as counseling or communicating to each other) and still aren't receiving the right amount of love and support in return, then you have the right to leave and to find someone who is willing to give you all of that and more.

Not all of your relationship-building will focus on your personal life: you will also have to use these skills in your professional arena. So how do you deal with unreasonable people? Unfortunately, many a person whom you will encounter in your life will be difficult to work with, or just plain hard to get along with. One reason for this could be that you have similar personalities and are unconsciously competing with each other. You may both be right, but you are both trying to get the upper hand about how the argument is worded, or about which path you should both take. This is common, and it's funny how people don't recognize it when it happens. I remember arguing with a close friend of mine for hours over a political argument. In the end, a third friend explained that we were both arguing about the same point, but seeing it through different lenses. For example: if one of us argued that lowering taxes would put more money into the pockets of the taxpayers and the other one argued that less government spending would lower taxes, the result of both of these viewpoints would equate to a similar result.

In order to deal with people like this, you have to be willing to allow them to lead the discussion and to feel like they are being heard. This will be difficult if he is the type of person who likes to take all the credit and makes you feel like a small part of the relationship. A better tactic is to work on compromising with him so that you can create a more productive relationship. If you can forge a great relationship with a like-minded person, then you can solve more problems by seeing if one of you can come up with something that the other person didn't think of. Learning to compromise isn't easy. People who have dominant person-alities want to be dominant; people with submissive personalities prefer to be led and will agree in order to avoid confrontation. It may be chal-lenging for you to build a positive relationship with either personality if the other person is unwilling to shoulder the burden of finding the best resolution possible. Finally, you can agree to not argue about certain things, and to only share information with each other when the situa-tion calls for it. This means that you won't be competing for who is right or who knows more; rather, you'll be conversing for fun, or to share knowledge in order to accomplish goals.

A second reason that people may be difficult to get along with may be that you have completely opposite views and see the world in different ways. Ideological differences can be tough to bridge. A vegetarian may have trouble understanding why people eat meat; Republicans may not understand the views of Democrats. These can be opinions that people developed via instruction from their parents, friends, or educators, or they could be the direct result of events that took place in their lives. Whichever side you fall on, your opinion will be strong, and occasionally unchangeable. Stay informed and don't fall for what some media outlets try to portray as the truth. Allow your own sense of reasoning to help make your decisions about what is right and what is wrong: just because people are affiliated with your party doesn't make them champions of your causes.

Consider fishing industry workers and environmentalists debating the ban of harvesting a species due to overfishing. The commercial fishermen's argument is that if they can't fish, then they cannot feed their families. The environmentalists argue that if they fish the species into extinction, their families will starve in the long run anyway, and the industry will collapse for an even greater period of time. It is not that either side is wrong; both have strong arguments. Logic tells you, however, that overfishing will have longer negative consequences than banning the harvesting of a species for a couple of years so that the environment can recover. But if you lay this logic out to the fishing community, all they will be able to think about is how are they going to be able to put food on the table. This is where a difference in opinions can lead to conflict.

Not everyone will want to reason and look for a solution that will be beneficial over the long haul. Most people want a quick fix, a sense of control, or to not admit that they are wrong; there is no use in arguing with these people. All it will cause you is stress, and it may lead to newer problems. You have to learn to compromise, to accept that you can't change these people, or to avoid them altogether.

A third reason is that you will encounter people who just plain don't like you for a specific reason, or for no reason at all. It could be that your behavior irritates them, or that they heard a rumor about you that they chose to treat as fact. Maybe you got the job a close friend wanted, or perhaps you scored the winning run in a softball game and stole the glory from her. Maybe you have a quality that a she is jealous of. Maybe she has an unpleasant disposition, and, no matter what you do, you can't win her approval. You can't make everyone happy, and the more you try, the less successful you will be, and the more stressed out you will become. The key here is to find the right partner to date, the right friends to let into your circle, the positive family members to spend time with, and the right role models to emulate. In this case, strive for quality over quantity. Networking is important, as I mentioned earlier, but if you feel that the only way you can succeed is by allowing negative people into your life, then you may not be putting yourself in the right position. You have to overcome your need to please people.

What if you find yourself in a situation where you have no choice but to deal with someone who seems to have it out for you? You have a couple of options. First, you can just accept it and avoid getting into arguments, while working toward putting yourself into alternative situations. If it's a temporary situation, focus on accomplishing your short-term goals. The quicker the group reaches its conclusion, the faster you can head back to your previous roles. If a person is unhappy in his current function, he could be in the process of looking to leave the group and/or organization. This could be the solution if you are part of a work or school team for a short period of time. Do your best to contribute to the group, and keep in mind that it will be over soon.

Second, you can kill these people with kindness, as they say. Go out of your way to do nice things for them or try to get to know them. With a little prodding, you can sometimes find out what they don't like about you, and either dispel their preconceived notions or alter your behavior to suit both parties. Sometimes people are introverts who hate change, and, once they get to know you, they might open up. Others may want you to prove yourself before they give you the OK. This won't always be the case; with some people, no matter how nice you are to them, they still may not be kind to you.

Sometimes it's best to take yourself out of the situation. Working with or being in a crowd with a person who makes you feel small is not good for you mentally or for the environment you share. You could develop anxiety or a physical ailment. The person may also cause problems for you in your workplace or at school by trying to make you appear inept or by influencing others to see you in a negative light. If you are in one of these situations and are unable to settle your differences alone, talk to someone who has control over the environment and explain what is going on. On the job, this would be a supervisor, manager, union representative, or human resources person. In a social setting, talk to the person who has the most sway. If your efforts go unrewarded, then it is best to move on. It's better to give your full notice and leave a job than to stay and allow your work performance and reputation to suffer. This could cause you to doubt yourself and take fewer chances in the future. You cannot let one person derail all your efforts or your self-esteem.

Alternately, don't abuse the kindness of people you don't know. As my niece was growing up, I always told her that you never know what values people have, so don't judge them until you get to know them. You'll encounter people throughout your life whom you naturally get along with or are attracted to in some way. I'm not saying to be best friends with a stalker, but I am saying to give people who want to befriend you a chance, because you never know how they can surprise you or what parts they may play in your future. You see this in movies all the time, where the character you think is shady or undesirable ends up being the hero and had good intentions that were not discovered until later on. This is why you should treat people with kindness until they give you reason to act differently.

CHAPTER 4

MENTAL HEALTH

DO NOT IGNORE this chapter. Your mental health is the foundation on which you build your sense of individuality and stability. This is important, because a weak structure offers little shelter in a storm. If you don't love yourself or have pride in who you are, then it will be nearly impossible for you to accomplish mighty goals and to endure all of the struggles along the way. I realize that this is not an easy task. Mental illness can wear heavily upon an individual and can make it impossible to feel confident and secure. You will pass over opportunities due to fear of rejection or your perceived inability to perform assigned tasks. This can cause you to self-isolate and miss out on important moments lurking around the corner.

What do you do if you feel like this? There are many ways to battle mental illness. I am a fan of self-realization. I internally break down what is causing my trouble and work through it; then I will be able to manage effectively on my own. For example, I have faced depression my whole life, and through writing and analyzing my words, I was able to identify my problems and to work to face them. While I don't feel I can be cured, it's become a manageable situation for me. I have learned what my triggers are, and I know the best ways to combat these spells of depression. Some people cannot overcome their problems on their own and may require counseling or even medication. Ignorance is not an excuse, and denial is not a solution. You have to have a fit mind to be able to grow and get the most out of yourself while building your foundation.

One tool for building a strong foundation is self-reflection. It may sound like a waste of time, but this was one of the ways I overcame many of my personal struggles. What is the point of self-reflection? It can help you truly understand the many parts of yourself, including how you see yourself and your world, what you perceive to be your obstacles, how you set and manage your goals, and what causes you to react to stressors in a certain way. Your bad decisions may be a product of something that was ingrained in you from youth. Your fears can be a reflection of past failures. Your lack of success could be a subconscious ploy to avoid being let down. I started to break myself down by writing poems and songs. At first I didn't understand why I wrote what I did, but after reflecting on the words, I saw common themes in what I had written. I identified symbols: when I mentioned the sun, it was generally a metaphor for me; when I wrote about rain, it symbolized sadness; and when I mentioned a window, it indicated that I was reflecting on something. Once I had made the connections between certain phrases or words and what they meant, I was able to see the hidden messages in each individual poem. This is how I began to understand what was bothering me and what the issues were that I needed to work through.

Another tool is having the ability to identify and embrace your strengths and weaknesses. This can be challenging, because you have to admit that you aren't perfect and that you have attributes that you need to work on and improve. Along the same lines, you may be hesitant to acknowledge that you are good at certain things because of fear that others will think you are bragging or not cool. If you are unaware of what your strengths are, then how can you identify them? You can start by asking questions like: What do I like to do? What am I good at? What subjects do I find interesting? What do people come to me for? Through seeking answers to these questions, you can forge a path and recognize a pattern.

Then you need to outline your weaknesses. Ask yourself what abilities you don't have confidence in: What am I afraid of? What do I dislike doing? Where have I failed to make progress, and why? List these weaknesses, and determine if there is a way to improve on any of them. If you aren't good at math but want to own your own business someday, what can you do to have a better understanding of basic algebra? Maybe you could take night classes or have a friend tutor you. Are you afraid of flying but want to travel the world? Is it something you can overcome? Take a short flight and see how you react. Do you dislike authority and need a job where you can be free to create and choose your own path? Are you qualified for any of these types of jobs in your field of interest that would give you that freedom? These are important things to consider.

You may notice that some of your strengths and weaknesses may conflict with one another. In this case, you have to decide if one is more powerful than the other. Do you have the ability to improve the weakness, or is it too profound to overcome? You may have to look to another one of your strengths. For example, you may be a great singer in private, but you freeze up when in public. You may practice in front of people every chance you get, but still not be able to conquer you phobia. If you cannot perform your art in a way that can sustain you professionally, then it may never be more than a hobby. I'm not advocating giving up on your dream, but if you also have a love for numbers, details, and organization, then you might decide to become an accountant. You can still try to advance your music in your private time and pursue your passions in other ways, but if you don't understand what you can and cannot do, then how can you expect to be able to make decisions that will be best for your future?

By using similar techniques to analyze yourself, you can start to look at ways to either reinforce your behavior or alter it. Good behavior should be reinforced. You often hear the phrase *low-hanging fruit*, which refers to reaching for objectives that can be easily reached. You may have a goal of a being a master chef, but get discouraged when you realize that you aren't a very good cook. You can reverse this notion by acquiring a couple of recipes and perfecting one dish at a time. Every effort you make to improve your situation will build your confidence and give you the courage to reach a little bit higher toward your goals.

Others may need to shake things up completely. While I was writing songs in my early twenties and struggling to pay my bills while working low-paying jobs, it became very clear to me that I wasn't getting where

I wanted to be. I had little confidence, allowed myself to do things that inhibited my ability to grow, and became trapped in my circumstances. I needed change. No one was going to come and save me, so I had to get motivated and stop wallowing in my disappointments. I chose to face my fears and break out of my comfort zone. I did this by quitting both jobs, packing up my truck, and heading out to California to pursue my music career. I had no idea where I was going or what would happen, but I didn't care. I desperately needed to change. This one act of pursuing my dreams was the first step in my becoming more confident that I could be something more in life. Even though I did not achieve my goal, that experience transformed me. No longer was I afraid to face my fears: I knew that I could take chances and that if I failed, I'd still be all right.

If you find yourself giving up or not putting forth an acceptable effort, then it's time to change your behavior. I noticed that when I conversed with people, I always gave my opinion immediately and dominated the conversation. I realized that this turns people off. Now I try to be a stronger listener and only add to the conversation when it seems appropriate to do so. This way, I have better conversations with people, and they feel that I am listening to them. While I was going to school, I realized I was a horrible presenter, so any chance I got, I volunteered to speak in front of people. You cannot improve on yourself if you continue to be afraid of your weaknesses: you have to identify them and take action to improve them.

It is also important to stay away from things that trigger bad behavior. You may turn to eating, drinking, or substance abuse when your problems become too much to handle. You may feel down and revel in bad feelings. Try to avoid these behaviors at all costs. You may need to combine many factors and build yourself a support structure so that negative events do not undo all the work you've done to get yourself ahead and in a positive place. You will likely lose a friend, a job, an investment, a car, even a pet, and sometimes all at once. You need to understand that things will go wrong. Prepare for that and avoid being afraid of challenging yourself as your situation gets tougher.

This is where you build your sense of resilience. As the walls come crumbling down around you, take a moment to breathe. Assess where you are and what you still have, and consider what you need to do to avoid losing more. You may have to take a step back and clear your head, seek help, or learn to accept things and let them go. You may have to change your career, or go back to school, but you cannot give up. You can't mask your pain with unhealthy habits. They won't cure your ills, and they won't improve your situation; they will only worsen it. If you give in to old vices, you could find yourself spiraling down even further.

When life challenges you, it's important to stay strong and self-assured. This is a good time to list all of your accomplishments and to believe that whatever you have done up to this point, you can and will do it again—perhaps even better the second time around. You should trust in your support system: your friends, family, spouse, mentors, and coworkers. If you need additional counseling, then get it. Do anything you can to avoid falling into the traps. Allow yourself to spend more time doing things you enjoy, like going for long walks, eating at a favorite restaurant, or getting wrapped up in a beloved hobby. Having a hobby (the subject of chapter 8) is important, since it can be a great stress reliever, give you material to talk about in conversations, and help add to your skill/knowledge base.

If none of this works, then volunteer at a soup kitchen or an animal shelter so that you can see that you aren't alone in your struggles and that others face similar problems. Volunteering also gives you a feeling of accomplishment and usefulness, and it allows you to interact with people or animals who will appreciate you for being there for them.

Another technique I have used in the past is to allow someone to mentor you. This sounds silly enough, but you'd be surprised how often people don't allow themselves to learn from others. I have always sought people who were knowledgeable and learned from them. You can't always judge a person who seems harsh or difficult. Personalities vary from person to person, and, by making quick judgments, you may lose the opportunity to build a useful connection. People act in different ways for different reasons. They might have had rough upbringings, they might have issues at home, they may be intimidated by you, or they might not understand that they come off as being harsh. Don't get me wrong, I understand that there are a lot of people out there who are hard to get along with, as we discussed in the last chapter. But if you invest a little time and effort, you may come away with a valuable relationship and a greater understanding of the ways to handle different personalities.

There's a line in the movie *Dune,* "Fear is the mind killer." This is so true. We are constantly evolving and taking on new and more complicated challenges. It starts when we are babies learning to walk and talk. Then we go to school and learn to socialize. As school progresses we learn about more complex subjects. Finally, we learn to drive. In high school, teens learn to play music, work with their hands in numerous trades, speak foreign languages, play sports, or study a whole wide range of other interests or skills. This is when you are able to see young people set themselves apart from others. Some work hard to get into college or develop skills so that they will be able to compete in the workforce. On the opposite side, others may not have taken advantage of their education and are left scared or unsure of what direction to take. A great many others will pick directions that are not their passions, but offer them some form of security.

For some, being an expert can be as much of a curse as it is a blessing. People who are gifted can be treated poorly by those who either don't understand them or are jealous that they can't reach the same level. People who are gifted can try to win these people over by showing them kindness or helping to further them in their passion, but if they can't be won over, or if they're unwilling to try, then it is best to let them go and move on. Everyone needs to surround themselves with like-minded people who will help them continue to grow. Be proud of your strengths, and embrace them. Realize that they make you special, and that they are gifts and not curses, even though it might seem like that at times. You just need to search for a place where you can freely exhibit your abilities, whether it be singing at a coffee house or teaching a class at a community college. These environments can give positive reinforcement and may reward you financially, socially, and/or personally. Don't let the fear of using your gifts force you to put yourself in a cage and isolate yourself. My gift was writing songs, but I allowed myself to get too deep sometimes, and the songwriting would feed my depression. Everyone needs time to breathe and think. If your gifts cause you anxiety, however, then you either need to talk about it with a professional or find a way to continue to excel without causing further stress to yourself.

When I ask, "Hey, what's your story?" many people just reply with a "Huh." Then I ask, "What are you about?" You'd be surprised how many people say nothing, and when I ask what they are good at, they say they don't know. This is a huge problem. Your skills and abilities are what will help you be successful and help you make good decisions. If you don't know what those skills are, then you need to spend some time self-analyzing, talking it over with a teacher or a boss you trust, or, even better, talking to a close friend. They may not be able to fully answer this question, but I bet they can get you started in the right direction.

So many people isolate themselves and fear taking on new challenges because they don't feel that they have any value. This could be caused by having been raised by parents who didn't have the right kind of skills to impart on their children, or they may have unresolved social issues that cause them to feel unwanted. It could be a combination of many other factors, including having undiagnosed mental issues, having experienced a one-time traumatic event that caused them to be stereotyped, or having grown up in the shadow of a sibling. The longer you allow yourself to be isolated, the more likely it will become the norm. If you become uncomfortable being around other people, then your self-worth and motivation can suffer immensely. Once you start sinking, you become desensitized to your situation, and the deeper the hole, the harder it is to get out.

Fear is the destabilizer and dream crusher of life. It will hold you back from applying for new jobs, taking a challenging class, or asking someone out for coffee. Every opportunity to grow is your chance to climb your ladder of success and to get closer to where you want to be. You have to be ready to face rejection and failure, knowing that you won't accomplish every set goal. Look at failure as an opportunity to gain knowledge: you can evaluate what went wrong and consider what improvements to make the next time you encounter a similar situation. Did you fail because you lacked knowledge or experience, or perhaps you didn't understand the situation you were in? This is common when looking for a job. Sometimes, for example, the company is looking for a particular characteristic or a certain level of knowledge. In that case, asking the right questions in an interview or requesting a follow-up interview is invaluable: if you know what you did wrong, you can prepare and build skills or knowledge for the next time.

While this sounds easy enough, the best way to work on beating your fears is to face them. If you are afraid to fly, book a flight. If you are nervous around people, then join a club. If you don't feel like you are very smart, take some night classes on subjects you find interesting. The only way to pop out of this bubble is to work on *you*. Identify your strengths and weakness, and *build* on your strengths and learn how to *minimize* your weaknesses. For example, two of my strengths are that I am creative and that I have a strong ability to analyze problems. So in writing this book, I am utilizing one of my strengths—my creativity. I am creating a piece of art that showcases my progression from someone who was lost and confused to someone who is strong and confident from overcoming various obstacles in life.

As mentioned previously, one of my main weaknesses is that I get nervous when speaking in front of people. My brain speeds up, I lose track of my train of thought, and I easily become tongue-tied. This is a problem for someone who once had a goal of becoming a high-level manager. Luckily, there were many situations where I could work on it, both in my job and while pursing my college education. Though it was challenging, I always took the opportunity to speak in front of people. By my senior year of college, speaking in front of the class was still not one of my strengths, but I felt less anxiety when doing so. I was becoming used to it. Repetition is one way to overcome fear: the less uncomfortable you feel in doing something, the better you will be at it.

People sometimes avoid giving themselves opportunities to do things like starting a new business or buying a house because of fear. If you are scared to make major changes in life, then you could be stuck continuing to work for a business that benefits from your hard work, but that you feel does not pay you fairly or give you the credit you deserve. Or, if you rent, you may feel angry that you are paying down someone else's mortgage instead of creating equity for yourself in a house that you own. When these people are told that they should look into being their own bosses or buying some real estate, they say, "Well, I wouldn't even know where to begin." The best way to get started is by doing research. You can look online and learn what's the best way to secure a loan, what classes to take in order to learn about the profession you are interested in, or if there are any government or assistance programs that could guide you. If you want to do something, you not only need to be brave enough to challenge yourself; you also have to arm yourself with the knowledge to be successful when you do take the chance.

Learning is a constant, never-ending process, no matter who you are or what you do. The more you learn, the more your brain makes connections. When you are well rounded and have a general understanding of how things work, you will doubt yourself less. Education doesn't just take place in a classroom, however. You can read books, join social groups, or go out and have experiences. Knowledge is power, and the more you equip yourself, the more powerful you will become.

Another essential ability is the ability to forgive. Learn to forgive your parents, friends, exes, and, most importantly, yourself. We are not perfect. We make many mistakes as we navigate our way through life. Some are intentional, and some are not. Some are made out of foolishness, while others are made out of ignorance. Some come out of pride, and so on. Sometimes we do something stupid and get so lost in the moment that we can't stop ourselves. And sometimes we're angry or even scared. We occasionally only see situations through our own lenses and we think we are doing our best to help, not knowing that our actions are bringing about the opposite reactions. We may not care, because the situation isn't that important to us at the time, or we are jealous and petty. This could result in you giving up on a friend, because you are afraid to be used or seen as weak. Maybe with a little help, that relationship could have paid high dividends. I've lost so many friendships through the years for ridiculous reasons. Sometimes I wanted to seem tough. Sometimes I felt that I was being used. Other times I just gave up because it didn't seem worth the energy at the time. My depression also caused me to isolate myself, or feel slighted even if it wasn't the case. I grew angry and would push away those I thought were offending me. Once in a while I found myself in situations where things were coming too easy to me and I overplayed my hand. This may have caused people whom I could have developed excellent partnerships with to walk away. Though I made many mistakes, so I had to learn to forgive myself. Those who really care will stay in touch.

Growing up as the son of a man who allowed addiction to dictate his life gave me further insight into this topic. I love my parents. I know that even though it's not always visible, deep inside that mess of a man is an honest, loving person whose decisions were clouded by a more powerful influence. All the decisions he has made, whether intentionally or not, have affected my emotional growth. His decisions affected my mother, my sister, and other family members, and set us all on a negative path. It is easy to harbor anger inside my heart and to blame him for all my shortcomings, but I can't. While he now understands that he made a lot of mistakes, he did what he thought was best at the time (even if it wasn't). And though I will always harbor some anger toward him and wonder what I would have accomplished had I been raised by someone who had invested more in his children, I can't take back what has been done. It's a waste of time to carry that anger.

Overall, he is still the same man he was back then, because he is still making the same choices. And if he could do it all over again, I am positive the results would be very similar. That is just who he is; it's the environment he grew up in, the people he surrounded himself with, the way his parents raised him, and his siblings' influence on him. All of these factors make a huge difference in how we turn out. Although my father didn't finish high school, and was never concerned about college, he was talented; anything he wanted to do, he excelled in. He didn't make bad decisions because he wanted to hurt people: he made them because he didn't know any better. By the time he knew better, he was resigned to accepting that it was too late to change. This does not vindicate him or his decisions; it only means that I see why he did what he did. I have to let that go. I cannot allow his demons to haunt me and to lead me to a similar place.

The way he treated me as a child directly contributed to my depression and the self-esteem issues I have battled throughout my life. I thought he hated me, and I hated him in return. No matter what I did, I never felt like I was good enough to be his son. I learned how to manage without his guidance or support and chose not to let that relationship define me. I took note of his mistakes and created my own path by trying to steer clear of the pitfalls he succumbed to. We cannot go back and change things; we can only look forward and hope to find a better way. And we should never give up. As long as there is breath in our lungs, we can strive for whatever we find important.

As I got older and more mature, I realized that the way he treated me wasn't my fault. I was never going to win his approval, because his mind-set was different from mine. He didn't believe in college, because he felt he wouldn't be a good student; he didn't understand my joy of playing in bands, because he couldn't see the value in it. He didn't follow sports, so we couldn't bond by discussing local teams. In short, we didn't have much in common. He didn't treat me the way I wanted to be treated because he didn't know how. I was a deep and analytical thinker, whereas he lived for the moment, without a care for tomorrow. We spent some time talking about this in our later years and made our peace with each other.

People will hurt you. You will get passed over for jobs, or you may even get fired. Friends will choose other people over you, and you will likely date a lot of people before you find the person who complements you. For the most part, people aren't trying to hurt you: they are making the best decisions they can with the information they have. Maybe they don't know or understand you. Perhaps they see some attributes in another person that are more attractive to them. Maybe they are being pressured or influenced by others. You will not be everyone's cup of tea. Everyone has a unique personality and no one can make everyone happy.

Once we understand what divides us from others (even the ones we care most about), then we can find understanding and even forgiveness. Not everything in life can be forgiven. There are things we cannot forget, and things people did that will hurt us in ways that will never heal. But if we can minimize these factors and let go of the pettier or more subjective arguments, we can find peace of mind. Anger will consume and destroy you. The less baggage you hold onto, the more love and understanding you will be able to give and receive from others. While this is easy to say, it's hard to do: you must train your mind, just like you would train your body. You can't let everything bad affect you in a long-lasting, negative way, and you must not take all of your perceived slights personally. You have to think, "Is this situation worth arguing over?" And you have to look beyond the situation to see if people are really trying to hurt you, or if they are just doing what they feel is the right thing. Once you incorporate this type of thought pattern, you can weed out situations that would have caused you stress in the past and work on the things that you know to be more serious.

If your life has been affected by a tragic event that you just can't seem to get over, then you need to be brave and take the time to deal with it. These can be either mental or physical events; whatever the case may be, don't allow them to fester and destroy you over the long run. Everyone eventually experiences an event that can cause anguish and restrict growth, whether it is experiencing an instance of mental or physical abuse, being involved in an accident of some kind, or facing a disease or ailment. I'm not saying that you should simply get over it and forget about it; I'm saying that you need to face it and then let it go, because you can't change what has happened. No matter how horrible the circumstances, remind yourself that you are still alive and that you have so much more life left to live. If you can't let yourself heal, then you are retarding your ability to get the most out of the rest of your life. You can use your bad experience to show others who may end up in similar situations how to overcome their own adversity. Or you can turn the past event into motivation so that you don't let your condition or the actions of another destroy the beautiful life that you foresee yourself living.

CHAPTER 5

PHYSICAL HEALTH

I KNOW THAT this sounds like a cliché, but many people still don't take advantage of the benefits this factor provides. Physical activity releases endorphins into your brain, which make you feel good and raise your confidence. Confidence attracts people and, in turn, enables opportunities to find you. When you feel good, that is one less obstacle on your path, which then leaves you free to worry about more important things. It's hard to consider this factor when you're young, because you are in the best physical shape of your life. As you get older, though, your body begins to break down. Those who smoke, drink, and abuse substances, or don't eat right, age quickly and can develop serious health problems. The older you get, the harder it is to change your patterns. That's why you should consider planning how to exercise, eat right, and limit the harmful things while you're still young enough to make a lasting impact on your health. That way, you can train these healthier behaviors to be automatic and easy to modify as needed. As you age, you may benefit by being seen younger as and more vibrant than you actually are. Good habits also aid in improving your mental health, and not only your physical health. When you feel good, challenges in life become easier to meet and resolve.

Your physical health is a gift. The freedom that good health offers you is irreplaceable. Older people pray to be young again; those who didn't take care of themselves when they were younger forever regret the effects. And people who have let themselves go will find it hard to get back to where they want to be.

If your goal is to become more fit or active, you have to retrain your body; this is comparable to the way in which you retrain your mind to improve learning. A lot of our problems stem from the food we eat. You can try to adjust your taste buds so that you will enjoy healthy food choices over those that contain fats, sugars, and salt. Take the stairs over an elevator, eat a banana instead of a hamburger, drink one beer instead of a six-pack, and say no to soda. It isn't easy. You may need to avoid eating at certain places, or avoid a few aisles at the supermarket to help resist the temptation.

If your goal is to lose weight, realize that it can be easier to drop five pounds than if your target is to lose a hundred. No matter the amount, you can achieve any goal you set your mind to and reach a weight that you will be happy with. For me, my target weight is my pants fitting. If they get a little tighter, then I know I have to step up my efforts. This is where having the right support system in place will come in handy: you will achieve greater success if you team up with people you know are into fitness and learn from them. Everyone has different methods and exercises they like to do. Some like to walk, some run, some ride bikes, some are gym rats, some get lost in sports, and others just keep busy around the house. It is important to explore different methods to find what the easiest way to keep you motivated is. For instance, I love nature and have really taken a liking to hiking. It's easy to get motivated to do this activity on a consistent basis, because when I am surrounded by plants, I feel like I can breathe better; I get a chance to observe forest residents such as deer, birds, and frogs; and I find the colors of brown and green to be visually stimulating. The world is getting smaller, and it's easy to feel claustrophobic with crowded roads, busy stores, and houses and apartments built so close to one another. In the middle of the woods, there is more space, and I feel free. I feel like I am visiting a small piece of heaven every time I'm out there. If you have a similar interest in being outdoors, every state provides a guide of land preserves, parks, or trails that you can go to nearby the city or town that you live in. Hiking also has physical benefits because it strengthens your leg muscles and gives you a good cardio workout.

Another exercise I enjoy is riding my bicycle around the neighborhood. Biking has many benefits. First, I can usually get a good workout, in a shorter amount of time than I would get from walking. Second, hiking too much can cause my knees to become sore. Biking is a way to continue working my legs daily, but at a lower level of impact on my body. Finally, I save money on gas by using my bike to go places a short distance away, like stores, parks, or friends' houses. Swimming also offers a low-impact exercise that is easy on your joints. Most areas have neighborhood pools or youth centers that will allow you access for a small fee. I also recently purchased a kayak and plan to add that to my routine; this adds to my love of being out in nature.

Finally, I do my strength training on a home gym; I also have a couple of sets of free weights, and I do push-ups to augment my routine. You may want to join a gym in order to have the ability to do similar versions of all of these exercises at one place and at one time. Going to a gym also allows you to be social, and it gives you the opportunity to meet new people who have common goals. New friends can offer you tips and ideas about how to manage your regimen. You just have to get it out of your mind that exercise is work: you can have fun with it.

There is a lot of knowledge out there, and there are a lot of programs to help you get into shape. Using the Internet allows us to ask any question we can think of and to get instant information. (Beware of sites that are trying to get you to buy a product or service.) We know smoking can cause cancer, hurts our lungs, and weakens every part of the body. Tobacco companies add all sorts of additives to cigarettes that make them more addictive and poisonous to our bodies. Why would someone want to smoke? As an ex-smoker, I admit I was done in by peer pressure. It took me eighteen years to stop. I was able to break the habit only with the help of antismoking pills. They help by robbing your brain of the ability to enjoy the cigarettes, and you slowly lose interest in lighting up. I told anyone who would listen how helpful these pills were, especially for people like me who battled this addiction for many years. Some of those people used this method to quit themselves, some quit cold turkey, and others denied that they needed to quit, or made excuses of why they couldn't. As they get older, I see their health deteriorating and their bodies weakening, and many of them can no longer participate in physical activities.

When I quit smoking, it took me a while to get back into shape, but my breathing slowly improved. I rode my bike and went hiking more often. I made changes to my diet. Through eating better and exercising more, I lost weight and gained muscle; I was in better shape in my thirties than I had been in my twenties.

Before I quit smoking, I was embarrassed that I smoked. I was self-conscious about my habit because I knew I was overweight. I had been athletic as a child, and I knew that I was losing the benefits of being healthy. Once I started to recover my health, however, I realized that even though I was older and I would never have the same abilities I'd had as a young kid, I could feel better, improve my mobility, and get back to looking and feeling good. Being healthy helped me be more confident in interviews and in my dealings with other people. I realize now that if I had maintained a healthier physical routine in my younger years, I would have taken more risks, I would have been more confident, and I would have made better decisions. Instead, I wasted too many beautiful days at home, sleeping, because I was hungover, or I stayed inside because it was hot out and I found it hard to breathe. I didn't join any teams or play organized sports because my body hurt too much.

It is crucial to know what you are putting into your body. It is well documented that you want to avoid sugary foods and soft drinks, stay away from white carbohydrates (such as white bread, white rice, and white potatoes), eat only a small portion of meat daily, and consume "super foods" (such as spinach, blueberries, and salmon) that contain higher levels of nutrients and antioxidants. It is also a myth that you can eat whatever you want when you are young and that it won't come back to haunt you later. This is because harmful foods can hurt your body over the long run; exposure to certain foods can lead to health problems down the road. The more meat you eat, for example, the more cholesterol can build up in your arteries over time; the more sugar you consume daily, the higher your risk for diabetes; and so on.

Another factor to consider is that over time, your metabolism slows down, and you will no longer be able to burn off all the calories you could when you were younger. The more weight you put on, the harder it becomes to take it off. This can lead to a loss in confidence, or it can limit your motivation. In addition, the fewer the nutrients in the food you consume, the hungrier you will become because you are not getting what you need to fuel your body. This is a lesson I have learned myself over the years. If you do not know which foods are good for you and which are not, however, then you may feel like you are eating healthily when really you are not. If you eat a salad but drown it in dressing that is high in fat and calories, then you are losing the benefit of choosing to eat that item. When you eat a piece of apple pie, you may think it is healthy because it contains fruit, but it is also high in sugars and carbohydrates.

The trick is to buy healthy foods you really enjoy in place of food choices you know are bad for you. For example, if you love fruit juice, then replace your soda with juice. Remember that fruit juices have a lot of sugar, though, so don't trade one binge drink for another. Make sure you check the labels and stick to brands that contain 100 percent fruit juice, since they will contain only natural sugars and the nutrients that your body needs. Use fruit juice as a reward instead of making it your main source of fluids; water should be your top choice for hydration. A hydrated body is a happy one: you will feel a lot better when you are hydrated, and it will keep your internal systems cleaner.

One major problem we all face is that we are always in a rush, and sometimes the quickest foods we find are not always the best ones for us. Avoiding fast foods at all costs will probably add years to your life, but the combination of fast, cheap, and convenient foods can be hard to pass up; this explains why fast food restaurants make a killing from selling their burgers and fries. How can we combat this? You may not be able to cut these options out altogether, but you can limit how much you consume by trying to find healthier options on the menu. You could also plan ahead and carry healthy snacks around with you in a purse or lunch bag. There is hope for us. The current trend is to bring healthier foods to the dinner table. Restaurants and supermarkets are aware of this shifting trend. Even McDonald's is devoting more of its menu to healthier options. Stop & Shop supermarket, whose headquarters is in Massachusetts, has a whole section dedicated to healthier food items, including frozen foods, a dairy/nondairy section, snacks, juices, and canned goods. Whole Foods Market is a chain of supermarkets whose mission is to supply people with fresher foods. Most supermarkets have sections in the store to offer either soy-based products instead of dairy or meat, organic foods with no GMOs or pesticides, and products with reduced sugar and fat content.

The problem with the health-food revolution is that you have to watch out for false advertising, and eating healthily can be expensive. Depending on your level of commitment, you should research companies to make sure they are living the values they preach. You also have to make sure that your cereal box doesn't claim that it is "healthy for kids" when in fact it is loaded with sugar and artificial ingredients that aren't good for children.

The economy isn't doing that well as of this writing. We are still experiencing a hangover from the 2008 recession, and most people can't afford to be health conscious. Most coupons found in newspapers and online are for food that isn't very healthy; you can generally stock up on these products more cheaply than with healthier alternatives. Fear sometimes comes into play, so that the shadow of starvation overcomes your good sense. You can combat this by planning out your meals and allocating funds to buy food in bulk. You can also grow food on your own. If you don't have a yard, then pick a spot on your back porch, plant some plants on a deck or near a window, or join a community garden. Being a part of a community garden can help you socialize and exchange tips. Every little bit that you grow not only gives you fresher, healthier foods, but cuts down on your total costs and gives you a new hobby and a sense of self accomplishment.

You might think, "Well, healthy food doesn't taste good," in which case you'll be under the illusion that you have to give up enjoying what you eat. You can change this perception by doing some easy research. Go online or purchase cookbooks for recipes that will help you learn how to prepare healthier foods without giving up taste. The more you focus on foods you already like, the easier it will be. Your taste buds will change and evolve as the food they process changes. A good example is that I like to drink green tea. It has a bitter taste to it, and every now and then I try different flavors. When I come back to the original green tea, it takes a couple of days before I start to prefer drinking it again. But once I do, I feel that nothing tastes better. Also, keep in mind that not all brands are the same. You may really enjoy some, but others may not be as palatable to you. Try different brands until you find the products that are right for you. Like everything, this is simply a matter of educating yourself, allowing room for learning, and taking chances until you can make proper decisions.

It is also important to have annual checkups with your doctor and dentist. The 2010 Affordable Care Act was designed to give more Americans the chance to receive the care that they need. More parents can keep their children under their insurance programs longer, and some conditions allow for receiving assistance for lower-income people. Whether you support this legislation or not, it is available, and, if you have the ability, you should utilize it. If you let medical problems go untreated for too long, or if you do not receive the preventative care you need, then it will be a lot more expensive and painful down the road when you decide to resolve your issues. As basic maintenance, you should get a physical once a year and your teeth cleaned twice a year.

Taking care of your teeth is important for multiple reasons. You use them to eat, they aid in your ability to speak, they don't grow back if they become damaged, and they are constantly in contact with bacteria. Some of the foods you eat can have negative effects on your teeth; for example, acidic foods can weaken your enamel, and sugary foods help grow the bacteria that causes cavities. Having a set of healthy teeth can keep your smile beautiful and can attract people, and you need to take care of them so that you don't lose them prematurely. This all ties in with confidence levels; although various technologies can replace your teeth, you obviously want to try to keep them as long as you can. Unhealthy teeth and gums can cause diseases such as gingivitis, as well as the weakening and cracking of teeth. Procedures such as implants, root canals, teeth pulling, and scaling (cleaning of the gums) can be both painful and costly. Even if you have insurance, some procedures may not be covered, or they might have high deductibles attached to them.

Getting a checkup every year helps you keep track of your blood pressure and cholesterol levels; while you're doing so, you can have screenings for cancer and other potential problems people have as they age. The earlier you detect a problem, the quicker you can combat it. Your doctor is also available to answer any questions you may have about minor conditions, provide you with advice on various medical issues, and inform you about proper diet and health in general.

Be aware of doctors who want to put you on medications, especially at a young age. I am not a medical professional, but it is my personal belief that through observation and experience, you can overcome many issues by changing your habits (or forming better habits) rather than taking drugs. Even prescription drugs have negative side effects: they can cause issues such as liver, kidney, or stomach problems. I had high cholesterol earlier in my life, and my doctor told me that I needed prescription drugs to combat the problem. I asked him to give me one year, and, through diet and exercise, I would try to reverse my condition. He agreed to let me take this course of action, but he advised me that some of my high cholesterol could be hereditary, and that there wasn't much I could do to change that. I came back a year later, and my cholesterol was back within a healthy range.

Another potential issue with too quickly accepting medications for solving health problems is that they could lead to addictions or cause you to become too reliant on the drugs. Your use of prescription drugs may start to mask your problems instead of solving them. Just because you receive a legal prescription doesn't mean that what you are doing is ethically or physically the right thing to do. When I had knee surgery, for example, I received a prescription for painkillers. By the time I finished the bottle, I had formed a slight craving for them; I used the last couple of pills as a sleep aid instead of for combating pain. I had a sense of relief when I took the last one, because I knew that I couldn't get any more and that I would have ended up forming an addiction had I continued to take them.

I also realize that not everyone has that type of willpower. Someone in a different situation may concoct another injury or tell his or her doctor that the pain was still there as a way of getting more pills. Since painkillers are narcotics and are highly addictive, the wrong person may obtain these pills illegally and move on to other drugs when the costs get too high, or a new supply gets harder to get. These types of addictions can happen quickly and without warning, and they can ruin families, careers, and lives.

I was addicted to cigarettes and I know how painful it is to quit an addiction that has become an embedded part of your daily routine. The substance tricks you into feeling that it makes you happy, and you get a combination of mental and physical pain when you can't get your fix. You may well think, "I would never be like that" if you have never experienced such addictions, but the dependence of these narcotics can overcome you quickly. People who become addicts start to make excuses about why they have to continue to use the substances.

This could be the case with more than painkillers. You could feel like you need medication so that you can still eat bad foods, continue to have poor sleeping patterns, or avoid dealing with stress. Stimulants and depressants come in a wide variety for everyday issues. If you have high stress and your only way to combat it is to take Xanax, for instance, then you aren't solving your stress problem: you are only temporarily avoiding it. You have to find out what is causing your stress and deal with that root cause. Whether it is a job, a person, an event, or even your residence, you have to isolate that factor and either learn to cope with it or move on from it. You may need to get a new job, end a relationship, or move to put yourself in a healthier environment. If you continue to mask the true culprit with medication, this may lead to other issues that could lead to serious conditions, such as having a heart attack or developing mental-health problems. Eliminate the problem. Do not ignore it and think that it will fix itself.

I'm not saying that this is possible for every case, and some people have conditions that cannot be improved without medication. I'm simply suggesting that you should try to be in tune with your body and take every possible course of action before settling on medication. Take my example above about needing pills to quit smoking. I smoked for eighteen years, starting when I was fifteen years old. I tried to quit for the majority of those years and failed every time. It wasn't until I had the aid of Chantix, a drug that stopped me from enjoying smoking that I was able to break free from that habit. Quitting smoking is one of my accomplishments that I am most proud of. When I was growing up, my parents, grandparents, family, friends, and nearly everyone else I knew smoked. I thought it was the one habit I could never free myself of. Once I quit smoking, I was able to start reclaiming a healthier lifestyle, and I returned to exercising and learning to eat right. That is why it was so important that I added these chapters to this book. Your physical health has a tremendous amount to do with your mental health, the way people perceive you, and your overall confidence. To summarize, it is important to be aware of your health, take preventative action, stay away from medications if possible (and use them only when absolutely necessary), and realize that your physical health affects every other part of your life.

Finally, I want to touch on drinking and recreational drugs. As of this writing, we are seeing a revolution in Colorado and other states where marijuana is being legalized. The argument is that pot is safer to consume than alcohol. This may be true in some ways, but it does not present the whole case. While the use of marijuana does have certain medicinal purposes and may benefit some people in limited recreational use, it is not a healthier alternative to alcohol. You are still inhaling carcinogens, and not only increasing your risk for cancer, but diminishing your lungs' capacity. Marijuana affects your brain cells and, with long periods of use, limits your ability to react and retain information. That's why they call it "dope," because it is known to kill off brain cells and make it harder for you to function at a high capacity. Getting used to abusing a drug, even one that is becoming socially acceptable, can lessen your opposition to harder substances.

Others claim that drugs can expand people's minds and aid in creativity. I can understand why there are two sides to this argument. Being under the influence can lower your inhibitions and can allow you to concentrate solely on what you want to accomplish. But you are risking your health and your brain power, and you are exposing yourself to habit-forming substances. The people you surround yourself with may encourage your use of drugs so that you fool yourself into thinking such use is acceptable. You may feel that you're merely rebelling or discovering hidden abilities, but the truth is that you are using a substance that will only hurt you over the long run. I can proudly stand behind these statements because at one time I felt the opposite. In time, as my habits changed, I watched others continue these behaviors into their later years. I realized that because we spent so much time glorifying this activity in our youth, some of these people never grew up and corrected their behavior. If you need to experiment and understand what it is all about, then that is your choice; I only ask that you don't get lost in the glamorization of it all. When you do move on to building your life, you have to learn to let these maladaptive behaviors go. Drugs don't make you great: what is in you is what makes you great. People have to reach that conclusion on their own. Unfortunately, some get lost along the way, and they never get the chance to realize that.

Drinking alcohol is a social norm. It is a way to socialize, meet people, make connections, and relax after a long day. Drinking also gets glamorized, however, and it can hurt you in the end if you allow it to get out of control. Limiting your drinking to a glass of wine here and a beer or two there can put you in a better position to partake in the advantages of social drinking, and when you do partake (in moderation), it will taste that much better. Unfortunately, a lot of people can't stop at a couple of drinks, and they get out of control. This is a great way to ruin friendships and working relationships, or even to get yourself into trouble with the law.

Some young people put too much stock into drinking in their teenage years. As they grow into young adults, they equate drinking with having fun. There seem to be few consequences for their actions, and drinking gives them a feeling of rebellion, or of being older and having control over their lives. Drinking affects people in different ways, however: some get happy, while some get depressed, and others may become violent. Young adults can turn to drinking when they hit low periods in their lives, as they associate drinking with having a good time. When they drink and realize that it is not giving them the desired effect that they hoped for, it can then lead to depression. Those who are still having a good time may not want to stop drinking because they are still enjoying it or are trying to hold onto their youth. This can affect people's personal relationships with their family, their friends, and their kids. The older a person gets, the harder it becomes to bounce back from partying. Just so, as your addiction to alcohol grows, it will start to cost you more and more. Your work performance will likely suffer, as will your physical and mental health. What started out as a fun thing to do on the weekend may become a permanent lifestyle.

When you are under the influence of any substance, whether drugs or alcohol, you have little control over your actions. Your reflexes become slower, your mind becomes hazy, and your judgment becomes clouded. While you may think you're being witty while you're under the influence, to someone who is sober, you might appear to be a jabbering fool. I have been on both sides of this situation.

This whole book is devoted to telling you about ways to make better decisions in your life that should help to make you successful and happy; it is not focused on taking sides on issues such as drinking alcohol, using drugs, or eating fast food. I am trying to cut through the layers of misconceptions and to get you to look deeper into the decisions you make that can affect your well-being. The goal is to enjoy your life.

Unfortunately, we are consistently swayed and persuaded that *this* is best for us, or *this* is cool to do, but you need to know both sides of every option. What are the positives? What are the negatives? How will this affect you in the short or long run? You will do whatever seems right at the time. I am giving you a guide to avoid the pitfalls that prevent people from reaching their full potential. I have fallen prey to many of the vices that I am warning you about, and, through those experiences, I have seen a better way that I want to share with you. Don't let anyone fool you. The truth is the truth, and the decisions you make are yours to choose. Just choose wisely.

CHAPTER 6

EDUCATION

PURSUING SOME LEVEL of higher education is now more important than ever. The majority of high school students go straight to college, and this creates a more educated workforce. Those who lack the proper degrees and/or levels of experience will find it difficult to obtain meaningful employment. The advent of globalization also puts a strain on those who are trying to enter the job market with limited skills or training. Even beyond that, we are also surrounded by so many new technologies and paths to education that if we don't keep working toward leading a life of continuous learning, we risk getting left behind. Countless studies have been conducted on the correlations between income, unemployment rates, and happiness, and how all of these improve as people increase their levels of education.

People don't pursue learning opportunities for a variety of reason. They may feel that they aren't smart enough, or that they don't have the resources or the time. They may have procrastinated for so long that their ambition becomes dulled. They may have attended schools that did not meet academic standards and did a poor job in teaching basic math, English, and science skills. They may have grown up in poverty and worked multiple jobs to help support their families. They may have been dissuaded by the cost of higher education and preferred not to incur large amounts of debt. They may have been poor students and felt that they would struggle with learning at a higher level. Maybe they didn't have the right friends, family, or student counselors to advise and support them. It could be that they didn't know what they wanted to do in life and decided to get a job instead. They may have gone directly into the military, followed in their parents' work trades, started families right out of high school, or spent their young adult years partying or traveling.

Everyone has the ability to learn. If you have a will, then you will find a way. It is never too late to go back to school and acquire an education. It always surprises me that some people think that they can't learn. Yes, some people have learning disabilities such as ADD and dyslexia, but colleges have implemented guidelines to help these students: they allow extra time for test taking and they offer on-campus tutors, and most teachers will spend out-of-class time to help students who need it. Colleges also offer lower-level classes as refreshers for those who may have been out of school for longer periods of time, or for those who may not have the ability to move into higher classes right away; there's also the option of auditing classes.

Learning is a constant thing. Even when a new phone or other device comes out, you have to learn how to use it. You may acquire a new recipe and decide that you want to change a few ingredients to improve the taste. You could be mowing or raking your lawn and think of a quicker way to get the job done. It could be that you are following a new TV program and you memorize all the characters and events. The point is that you are always learning. Lower-level classes are designed to build on your knowledge base so that you will be more prepared as the workload becomes more challenging later on.

The problem with higher education is that a large price tag is associated with it. If you don't have any money, then how can you sign up for classes? The most common method is to apply for student loans. You can get money for books and classes and not have to worry about paying it back until after you receive your degree. You can generally get low rates and manageable payments. The downside is that you graduate with a large amount of debt, and over time, interest rates can increase and leave you exposed to predatory loan consolidation companies. Another way you can pay for classes is to save up or use your credit card to take only a couple of classes at a time. This way, you can manage your debt as you go. This strategy can strain your finances in the short run, however, and will increase the length of time it takes you to graduate. You could also apply for scholarships from your school, from corporations, or through the government; these could help lower your overall costs. Finally, you may want to look for an employer that offers education reimbursement. This will not only lower your overall costs, but you will already have your foot in the door and will be able to take advantage of better opportunities once you graduate.

Some people never go to college because they didn't go immediately after graduating from high school and now feel that it is too late. I started college at the age of twenty-seven and graduated at thirty-eight. I went to school with students as young as seventeen and some who graduated in their sixties. The longer people have been away from school, the more they start to question their ability to return to school and to perform at a high level. I found this to be untrue. Students that return after spending some time in the workforce generally have a higher level of appreciation for the opportunity. I, in particular, found that real life experience in a corporate setting helped me to better understand most of the material I was learning. Some start families and feel that it is too difficult to manage between their family lives, work, and school. The more you have going on in life, the more difficult it becomes—but it is not impossible. Create a schedule and figure out a way to manage the most important factors in your life. If you can make and adhere to a set schedule, you can find a way to manage all of your priorities effectively. (For guidance, please reference the scheduling tool at the end of this book.)

Another plus is that when you further your education, you do it on your own terms: while of course you still can't be disruptive in class or cheat, you do have control over how you perform. If you don't want to go to school, no one is stopping you: you can stay home if you want to. I would advise against this, however, because college represents accelerated learning, and the more you miss, the easier it is to fall behind. Second, your performance only affects you. Teachers are paid by your tuition, and though it looks good for them to pass as many students as possible, they will let you fail. It is up to you to do the work. Of course, a lack of effort can lead to you failing the class and having to pay more money to retake it. Finally, you have control over what you decide to learn. Whereas in high school you have to follow a set curriculum, in college, you pick a major, and you can also pick a minor and have some say over your electives. Your major is your main area of study, and your minor is like having a secondary skill; this allows you to apply for more jobs, since you have a record of studying in multiple fields. For instance, if you major in information systems and minor in accounting, you can use accounting as a fallback job if you struggle to find employment in the information technology (IT) field.

Once you decide that you are interested in advancing your education, I would advise that you do some research. Don't just pick a major because it sounds fun or easy. Pick something that you love and find interesting; that will make it easier for you to study and retain interest in your course work. A school adviser can give you some insight into the different subjects and can help you match your interests with the right programs. Second, make sure you find a university or school that has good programs and teachers. You can now look online and see how students rate professors and get a general feel for students' experiences. It's one thing for a class to be easy, but if the teacher isn't effective in sharing knowledge with you, then even showing up for class will be a waste of your time. You can also visit schools and talk to faculty members, advisers, and current students. You are spending your money to get this education, and you should take pride in your work and be motivated to get the most you can out of your investment. Finally, make sure that jobs are available in the profession you want to enter. Although there are always exceptions to the rule, nothing is worse than sinking tens of thousands of dollars into debt only to find that you cannot get a job, or that the field you're in isn't worth the money you spent for the degree. You also don't want to get trapped in a dying field with limited opportunities.

You can take classes in a variety of different settings. The first thing you want to do is to undo the perception that you have to go an expensive university, surrounded by young, pampered college students who spend their time partying. Many older students return to college because they lost their jobs, they need degrees to get promoted, or they are at a point where they can (and want to) take classes for the sake of learning. Because of this, colleges are starting to focus on students of all ages. They offer classes at different times of the day (some schools offer weekend classes) and are increasing their online offerings. Accelerated classes are also beneficial because they allow students to complete more classes in shorter periods of time, and they speed up the path to graduation. The downside is that students have to pay for more classes in that shorter time frame, and they also have to endure longer class times and process more information in shorter periods of time.

If your preference is to learn in a classroom setting, then you have a couple of options to choose from. Community colleges are generally located in more populated areas, are less expensive, and are geared toward students of all ages; they are more flexible in their offerings, class times, and locations. They also have a large number of adjunct teachers who are enthusiastic and teach for the love of teaching. Most people go to community colleges to earn their associate's degrees (two-year undergraduate degrees). Students at community colleges may use these schools as a platform for improving their skills before moving on to a university, or to earn credits toward a bachelor's degree at a lower cost than at traditional four-year institutions. Credits earned at a two-year university can easily be transferred to other institutions. Be aware, however, that not all credits from your associate's degree may transfer over to your bachelor's program, so be sure to check with a degree adviser if you decide to pursue academic work at a four-year institution.

At state and private universities, you can earn a bachelor's degree, or you can continue your studies in order to obtain advanced degrees such as master's or doctorate degrees. State universities are more widely dispersed across the United States than their more elite counterparts; they are easier to get accepted into and are less costly than private schools. Private universities are more difficult to get into, and you may be required to submit extensive essays and to have high SAT scores and a list of other accomplishments. While they are more expensive, you also get a higher level of education. The better the school, the more prestige your degree holds. As with any profession, top schools recruit the best teachers so that the schools can attract the brightest and best students. You should be able to get a valuable education, no matter what school you attend, but do your research: sometimes you get what you pay for.

Taking classes on school grounds offers many valuable benefits that may be difficult to obtain if you are taking online courses. This really depends on your learning style. The teacher is right there in the classroom, and you can ask questions right away if you are struggling with any of the material. The teacher may also be able to afford you extra help before or after class, and can sit with you to work on any extra problems you may be having trouble with. You can network with other students and either build friendships or have access to people who can help you with the classwork. Working in real-life groups can gain you firsthand experience with working on projects with people who have different ideas, personalities, and ways of approaching problems than you do. You can observe what motivates people, and you can test methods for improving communication and teamwork with difficult people. Another benefit of attending physical schools is that most academic facilities have libraries and computer rooms onsite, so that you will have the resources to do classwork and research. This is helpful if you don't have the resources at home, or if you have to compete for computer time. You can also have more access to advisers and tutors.

One downside of classroom learning is that classes are on set schedules, and real life may not be accommodating, which can lead to various conflicts. Second, you have to travel, and that can be difficult during rush-hour traffic, or if you live in an area where it snows a lot. Finally, other students in the classroom can affect your learning by being disruptive (for instance, by texting friends or watching videos during lectures), or you may have to team up with people who may not take their education as seriously as you do.

Online classes are becoming more and more popular; these days you should have no trouble earning most basic degrees online. Taking classes in this way can have many benefits, but it also has its drawbacks. First, it allows you to manage your class time around your schedule: if you work at night, for instance, you can do your classwork in the morning, and if you work in the morning, you can do your classwork at night. Second, instead of having to drive to class, you can get right to work on your computer. Third, in the physical classroom, teachers often spend the class lecturing rather than working on more interactive exercises that will build your knowledge; then, after class, you still have to go home and work on the assignments they give you. Taking online classes allows you to cut through these different layers of education. Fourth, online learning can give you a sense of independence, but it does limit your face-to-face interactions with other students (which, if you are an introvert, you may really enjoy). While having such independence can be a plus, you may miss out on the opportunity to learn how to effectively work with difficult people in person, which can be a useful skill in the business world (although a lot of business is now conducted online, and you must also be able to solve issues via chat or e-mail). Finally, you can do online work at any location: you can do it at home or at the library or at a local coffee shop—wherever you feel like you can concentrate and obtain the correct resources to get your work done.

Furthering your education can be done in other ways other than getting an accredited degree. Many certification programs are out there that can lead directly to careers in industries like the medical and technology fields. You can find these programs at community colleges, universities, and other online institutions. They are generally less expensive and are of shorter duration than traditional degree programs, since the main focus is on learning a specific set of skills. Because of this, you miss out on the opportunity to take noncore classes such as history, science, or art that are unrelated to your certification. While some would say this is a good thing, I think it detracts from your overall educational experience. Whatever you choose to do, it's important that you check the job market for the occupation you are working toward, since some of these jobs may be low paying and may limit your career path. Because you will still have to put in the time and money, make sure you are getting good value for your expenditure. You may have earned your certification for starting a career, but you may find that the available jobs are not as rewarding as you thought they would be. At this point, you have to try to find other ways to increase your opportunities, such as furthering your education or starting your own business.

Another career path you can choose is to go to trade school in place of (or following) high school. Many skilled professions are currently understaffed that can make for fulfilling careers. Basic trades are being overlooked as more and more parents try to push their kids into what they feel would be a better life of using their brains instead of their bodies. Due to the increasing loss of basic skills that were once passed on from generation to generation, people who go into trades now have great opportunities to find financially successful lives. Some of these trades include plumbing, electrical work, HVAC, and carpentry. There will always be a need for these types of professions; it is important for tradespeople to continue learning in order to keep up with trends and changing technologies.

Not only can education help you in the job market; it can also be empowering. It helps you realize that you can do things you never thought you could do. I can't say for sure how much I retained from all the classes I took in college. It went by so quickly, and I was always clearing my mind to make room for the next semester's classes. What stays with you is the *ability* to learn. You also benefit from gaining improved cognitive function, from understanding the connections between different subjects, and from reducing your fear of being challenged. In your first couple of semesters, you will ask yourself, "How will I ever understand this?" As the semesters pass, however, you'll realize that there's nothing you can't accomplish with a little effort.

The best way to succeed in an educational setting is to understand the importance of time management. You have to make sure that you have enough time to process the material and to be able to produce acceptable outputs. You have to make sure you put enough effort into your studying, homework, and reports so that you will fully understand what the subject is about. The more you can retain, the more you can build on your knowledge base. If you don't have good study habits, then you will most likely be under duress and always rushing to finish your work. This will make it harder to get a good grasp on your subjects. If you get used to producing subpar work, then you risk developing bad habits that may carry on into your professional life. In college (where you or your parents are paying for your education), doing poorly will only hurt yourself. If you are having trouble with any subjects, then there are many ways to get help. You can look online, seek tutoring, ask fellow students or friends who are in the class, or you can ask your adviser for advice about how to get help.

Sometimes success is entirely related to perception. I went to college knowing that this was my chance to be something in life. I worked hard in all of my classes and made sure that I challenged myself. I took this as an opportunity to identify my strengths and weaknesses, and I learned how to improve on them. Taking electives and noncore classes helped open my mind to other subjects that I may not have had an interest in or a strong understanding of. In music appreciation class, for example, I learned about famous composers like Bach, Beethoven, and Mozart. I studied art terminology in art appreciation class, and I learned about how artists' styles can differ in factors such as color use, shading, and lighting. I had always wondered how artists like Picasso became so famous, since his artwork seemed childlike to me. After studying his work, I learned that he was bored with doing lifelike paintings (which he had mastered) and wanted to challenge himself beyond the accepted methods in order to become a more creative artist. On the opposite side of the spectrum, I took a class on Excel, which served me well in my later jobs doing charts and graphs. I took an environmental science class that changed my perspective on the things I bought and ate, and taught me how I could affect the environment in positive ways with a few simple changes to my habits: for starters, I began to recycle more and to use reusable bags. These and other small changes can have large impacts over time. I took a literature class and read several great works, including Dante's *Inferno* and Li Po's poetry.

The reason I mention all this is because a lot of students don't see the value of noncore classes. I think such classes help to add value to your education and make you a well-rounded person. They help you understand the basic concepts and themes of different topics, and they help you share your thoughts, converse with others, and learn more about yourself and others.

Again, I want to state that you must not be afraid to challenge yourself. These are learning environments where, although people may be coming from different walks of life, they are all trying to achieve the same goal of earning a degree, working toward a license, or obtaining a certification. High school and college are great places to begin to test and increase the limits of your abilities. For instance, I took a public-speaking course and was frightened because, as I've mentioned, this has always been a weakness of mine. I realized during that semester that most of the other people in the class were just as nervous as I was, and, because of this, we were supportive of one another. This helped me feel more secure when I spoke in public, because my fellow students weren't expecting me to be perfect; they simply wanted to see that I was exerting the same amount of effort as they were.

By the time you are ready to graduate, you will have worked with some students who have excelled and others who have failed, but I have learned that if you give something your all, then you are likely to do well, even if you are not strong in a particular subject. If you are not afraid to put in the time and hard work, then you can vastly increase your opportunities by pursuing subjects that you may feel are out of your realm of comfort—but that can lead to exciting jobs and experiences.

CHAPTER 7

INVESTING

A TEACHER ONCE told me that you should "pay yourself first." I believe he put the figure at 20 percent of your earnings. Realistically, most of us cannot do this; we can maybe set aside 5 or 10 percent. Whatever we set aside, it should be an amount we feel comfortable saving. Even beyond saving, we need to invest our money in order for it to grown. Inflation can quickly eat up people's savings, and, in ten years, their net value could be considerably less than it is today, even though the actual amount of money they have has increased.

We are taught to value money, but it goes fast. You buy a car, you buy a house, you furnish a house, you have a child, and all of this slowly chips away at your nest egg. It helps to talk with a financial adviser and to set up a diversified portfolio. You should have stocks and bonds, but remember that some investment methods are safer than others. Property, precious metals (for example, gold and silver coins from the United States Mint, and jewelry), and other collectibles (such as art and sports memorabilia) are things that you can purchase and enjoy now, but will also add to your total net worth as they appreciate over time. You cannot be afraid to think about your retirement when you are young. Life goes by fast, and the cost of living increases each year. Failing to develop the discipline of saving in your youth can hurt you considerably in the future.

If you have trouble saving money, one effective method is to utilize direct deposit. Most employers offer this service for free. Have a certain sum of money taken out of your check each week and deposited into an account in a bank or credit union in a location that is hard for you to get to. Do not get a debit card, so that you will only be able to access this money if you physically go to the bank. By not having easy access to this money, you tend to forget about it, and it will build over time without you even realizing it. For example, if you save fifty dollars a week, in one year you will have saved $2,600. This is a great down payment for a car, or part of one for a house. Maybe you'd rather start a personal trading stock account, or to sign up for a couple of college classes.

That brings me to another good decision, which is to invest in property. Ownership helps you whether you are the resident or a landlord. Either way, the resident of your property pays down your loan and increases your equity. True, when you own a property you have to spend more money on upkeep and repairs, but, over the long run, it will still be cheaper than paying a larger amount monthly to a landlord. Any improvements you make to the property help it hold its value and potentially increase its value over time (depending on market conditions). Every wall you paint, every shrub you plant, every rug you place builds pride in your home and gives you a feeling of accomplishment and security. Many people fear making such a large investment. As with your car, if you treat it well and maintain it, you will get plenty of usage out of it over time, and when you are ready to sell, you will get something back from your investment.

For your first purchase, make sure to buy something within your price range; perhaps a small house or condo would be appropriate to start with. If you can, try to put down at least 20 percent of the purchase price. This could lead to better rates and help you avoid having to take out loan insurance. Second, make sure that purchasing this home won't use up all of your disposable income. Unexpected bills will pop up, taxes increase yearly, you may need to redo the driveway or the roof or to buy a new car, and you may want to go back to school or start a family. If the house you buy sucks up all of your income, then you will be hard-pressed to accomplish any other goals. You may be forced to overuse your credit cards and thus get yourself deeper into debt. This, in turn, can ruin your credit and can make any further expenditures impossible. Even in desirable (i.e., expensive) towns, you should be able to find affordable foreclosures, fixer-uppers, or smaller houses that are appealing to first-time buyers. Every house you purchase will need some improvements, so don't be afraid to buy something that needs a little work: just make a list of the most important things that need to be done and tackle them one at a time. As the years go by, you'll be amazed at how beautiful you have made your home. As your wealth increases, you can upgrade. Maybe you and your spouse's incomes have doubled, or you have paid down a good share of the loan, and now you want a larger house. You can then choose to sell your first house if you feel there is a good profit to be made, or rent it out and let someone else increase your equity in the property.

I also want to briefly discuss car ownership, especially for young people who are just beginning to drive. Spend more and get a better car, rather than spending less, thinking the car you are buying is just temporary. Older cars with more problems will cost you more in the long run by needing more repairs, being less fuel-efficient, and potentially leading you to miss work or other opportunities for making money. Like everything in life, the more you invest, the better quality you get.

Stocks and bonds are also excellent ways to invest. As interest rates go down, put your money into stocks. And as they rise, put more money into bonds. While bonds can be safer than stocks, with less risk comes less reward. Stocks are less certain to increase in value, but if you play them right, you can receive big gains. Some stocks give you a quarterly dividend, which is a percentage of the stock price in cash; a dividend can be anywhere between a couple of cents to several dollars per share. If you manage your stocks by yourself, try to stay with "blue-chip" companies. These are top-rated companies that have well-earned reputations for excellence. The stronger the company, the more opportunity it has to sustain its growth by spending money on research and development in order to bring new products to market. These companies can also rely more on brand strength to retain customers and offer shareholder returns.

You should also invest in current trends. If health foods are popular, see what companies dominate the health food aisle in your supermarket; if a new technology is dominating the headlines, see what companies are involved with that industry. Be careful not to get too excited about new technologies, however, and make sure you do your research before investing. While I believe that solar power and stem cells are the future (and they may well be someday), the stocks I invested in told a different story.

Invest in the 401(k) or other retirement plan that your company offers as soon as possible. If the company matches a percentage of your investment, you should start with at least that amount. Failure to do so can mean giving up hundreds or even thousands of free dollars every year, which will add up to a lot of money over the long run. Retirement-plan contributions are also tax-exempt, and they lower your taxable gross income, which means that you will get more back from the IRS every year—just for contributing to your retirement. If you are uncomfortable making your financial retirement decisions, most financial companies offer services to manage your accounts for a small fee. Consider using experts with your money, because they have insights that can help you grow your money more than you would be able to on your own.

Starting a business may be a great investment if you have a defined skill that is in demand. If you are a plumber, for example, you may be able to make more money on your own than from working hourly for someone else. If you are a chef, you might want to consider opening your own restaurant. If you come into some money, you may want to look into purchasing a franchise of some kind. Because a large percentage of businesses do fail, make sure that you do your homework and see if the market you are trying to penetrate has the potential for growth.

I have watched many people spend their money because they felt there was no need to save. Then, when hard times come around (as they inevitably do), they are left in the lurch and have trouble keeping themselves on stable ground. Money is nice, and we all enjoy status symbols like having nice cars, clothes, electronics, and such. But if you spend your money as quickly as it comes in, then what will you do when the rough times come? We live in an ever-changing economic environment. Students who are coming out of college are having a harder time finding employment, companies are trying to run "lean and mean," and jobs are always moving to where the labor is cheaper. The global economy has changed the prospects for most people. As a local economy strengthens, the people in that region are able to afford more, and the more they can afford, the more they want. Companies realize that this labor stream is too expensive, and they may choose to downsize or relocate, and the economic boom in that area becomes a bust. You can compare these situations to the California Gold Rush that took place in the mid-1800s. Towns and cities were built and many fortunes were made, but when the rush ended, many of those places were abandoned and the store owners went out of business.

You have to prepare for the future as much as you enjoy the present. By putting money away, you can create more opportunities for yourself, and as your savings increase, you can make larger investments. Instead of a small house, you can buy a midsize house or a piece of land. You can invest in stocks that are more expensive and in their prime, such as Apple or Google, and that thus have the potential to make larger profits. You can pay cash for a car straight off the lot and not pay double the cost in interest over the next five years. Money makes money.

Along the same lines, having extra money helps you in times of crisis. What if you own a house and a pipe bursts, flooding your basement and ruining your furniture, and you need to pay a ten-thousand-dollar repair bill? What if you lose your job or find out that your family is growing? Having sufficient funds protects you from an immediate financial crisis; it gives you the flexibility to handle situations as they come and to prevent them from getting worse. What if all of these events happened to you in the same week? If you only had a few hundred dollars in the bank, this could cause you extreme anxiety, and might cause you to make unwise decisions. For instance, you could start drinking to help you cope, take your anger out on your spouse, or become depressed and feel helpless. None of these suggestions will make life any better. If you had fifty thousand dollars in the bank, on the other hand, you might think, "I can finance some of these repairs and pay for the other half right now. We have some money to pay the bills while I search for a job, and we still have enough to pay for some of the medical costs, so we can begin to buy items like a car seat and diapers."

That peace of mind can be the difference between falling into a rut and avoiding that rut completely. Your safety and small sacrifice of putting away a hundred dollars a week instead of buying a new pair of sneakers or getting a more expensive car really can make the difference. Your peace of mind is not just related to having money; it means having control and the ability to handle situations that will help you avoid the pitfalls that come with being unprepared.

Another way that people get themselves into trouble is by relying too much on credit cards and by blindly using their debit cards and store credit cards. When you do this, you get the sense that you have a lot of buying power, when in fact the bank may have given you far more credit than you can afford to pay back. When you only make the minimum payments, you incur interest rates, and that ten-dollar blouse could end up costing thirty dollars by the time you pay it off. While it is important to build up your credit, you need to do it wisely: only buy what you know you can pay off in a short time, and do not get into the habit of using your credit cards when times are tough. Going back to the example of the triple crisis I used before with the burst pipe, the lost job, and the unexpected pregnancy, if, out of fear, you start putting everything on your credit cards to get by, you are actually creating a worse financial situation: you are creating more debt by charging a large amount of money that you do not currently have the resources to pay off. In the long run, this can destroy your credit, take you longer to recover, and drive you deeper into a sense of panic or depression. Another thing to keep in mind is that some companies now do credit checks when they hire people, and failing such a check could cost you a potentially great job.

Failure to properly invest will hurt you most in your golden years. If you are unable to set yourself up properly, you may struggle to live comfortably in your advanced age. Those who invested wisely, in contrast, will most likely own a home that is paid off (or close to it), thus eliminating a major expense. Those who saved a portion of their earnings will be able to survive off some of their investments, 401(k) plans, or savings. If you purchased multiple properties, you can either sell or rent them out for extra income; if you diversified your investments, some may have failed, but others may have exceeded your expectations. You can then retire in comfort and security knowing that you and your family are well cared for.

If you did not invest wisely, you may face an uphill battle. The older you get, the harder it is to find meaningful employment. People are naturally prejudiced for many reasons, and age is a major one. Hiring managers may look for employees who are younger and more energetic, even though older people may have more ability and experience. You may be forced to live in debt or accept a standard of living that is below what you are accustomed to; you may have to sell off everything you have acquired just to pay the bills. You may have to rely on family to help support you, which will then cause them to resent you, or will strain those relationships. The longer you wait to make good decisions, the more the odds are stacked against you being able to live a fulfilling life.

Always invest in yourself. Wear the right clothing for interviews, and, if you get hired, dress for success. People look at you and judge you by your appearance; this is unavoidable. Invest in your education, because the more you know, the more advantages you will have in competing for jobs. If you enjoy art and are knowledgeable about it, by all means, invest in art. Invest in what you know about and what you enjoy; even if you don't make tons of money, at least you will have a hobby that you enjoy that will also improve your mental health.

CHAPTER 8

HOBBIES

WE ALL NEED hobbies. They are our means of escape from stress and the doldrums of life. Many studies have shown that video games can actually teach people skills that are valuable in the workplace. This is not me validating a video-game addiction, but recognition that hobbies can enhance your life. Being able to funnel your passion into an activity that you can share with friends or family members is a wonderful thing that helps to strengthen relationships, friendships, and your mental health. You can also use your hobbies to build wealth by becoming a collector, whether your hobby is in art, historic items, or even comic books.

Hobbies are also healthy activities because they help you structure your time. When you come home from work or school, if you have nothing planned, then more often than not you will likely sit around and watch TV or surf the Internet. Instead, you can use that time to join a softball team and get some physical exercise, or you can spend some time researching stocks you might be interested in. We always say we'll look to tomorrow, but life is short. There are 365 days in a year, and if we live to eighty, that means we have 29,200 days to live. The average person spends eight hours asleep, eight hours at work, a few more hours driving and getting ready to do things, and that means you have less than one-third of your life to enjoy yourself. This leaves approximately 233,600 hours. While that seems like a lot of time, it really is not. Think of it as money. While $233,600 seems like a lot of money, as you start pulling chunks out of the pile, it goes really fast. Don't waste your time thinking, "If I did this," "I wish I could go here," "I wish I learned this or that." Go do it. Live your life and take advantage of the fact that you can do anything you put your mind to.

A lot of studies have shown that video games are actually a great way to educate students. They help people solve complex problems, work in teams, build relationships, and accomplish goals. It's easier to engage students when they think of learning as being fun and exciting. They will be more willing to take on greater challenges and embrace team-work, which is essential in succeeding in real-world jobs. Game-playing can also help those who are shy or who struggle with their self-confidence; it can show them that they do have the talent to perform well and be embraced by others. They might find it easier to take on real-world challenges because of the success they had playing these games. Keep in mind, though, that this can also work in reverse: those who find that they are successful in virtual worlds may have a hard time adjusting to the fact that they are only average in work-place scenarios. Others may get a taste of failure or rejection in a real-world situation and desire to return to the imaginary world for comfort, and some may not want to venture out and take risks at all. Having real-life jobs or relationships also may not give them the same thrill, challenge, variety, or comfort that playing games may give them.

I also recommend learning how to play chess. It's a very old game, but still has many lessons to offer. Earlier, I discussed good ways to ana-lyze your strengths and weaknesses and to improve upon them both. Chess has similar qualities. The pawns are limited in movement and are not highly valued; the horses (knights) only move in L-shape patterns. The bishops stay on their own colors (i.e., black bishops must stay on black squares) and they can only move diagonally. The two powerful rooks on each side can only move in straight lines vertically or horizon-tally across the board. Then there is the highly prized queen, who can move in any direction she wants and is the key piece to many players' success. Finally, you have the slightly less powerful king, who can also move in any direction, but only one square at a time; you must keep the king out of harm's way, or else you'll lose the game. The key to winning is to learn and utilize the strengths and weaknesses of all the pieces, even the pawns. Each opponent you battle has the same exact pieces at his or her disposal, but will have attained varying sets of skills. As your proficiency increases, you will master the art of using your pieces in unison with the dual goal of protecting the king while trapping your opponents. The game sharpens your mind, as it takes a lot of concentration to keep track not only of your own pieces, but of the movements of your competitor. Meanwhile, your opponent is trying to misdirect you in order to get you to weaken your defenses and to create opportunities to strike. Some of the finer points the game can teach you include learning how to sacrifice pieces to lure your opponent into traps, how to retreat and fortify your defenses if your competitor has gained the advantage, and how to overcome mistakes in order to reach your goal of winning the match.

The more I play chess, the more I realize how much it mirrors life. You begin to recognize patterns in the way you play: Are you aggressive, or do you prefer to take your time? How do you react to adversity: Do you give up easily, or do you become stronger? Does it take a challenge to fire you up, or do you come prepared to win every time? Once you realize how you approach challenges, you can develop your strategies. Since you have an array of pieces that possess different skills and abilities at your disposal, it's important to learn how to complement each piece's strengths and to cover up their weaknesses in order to increase your chances of success.

After playing for a couple of years, I started to notice that players tend to favor certain pieces, whether it be their knights, their rooks, or their queen. These players can be defeated more easily than players who don't favor particular pieces, because once you take that piece away, their game suffers. In order to become a better player, you must challenge yourself during games to win using other pieces. Developing your ability to win with lesser pieces means that you can still compete even when you experience a misstep. This is the time when you learn that patience is more advantageous than pure power. One of your most plentiful pieces is often overlooked: the lowly pawns, which offer the least amount of ability (and mobility), can become extremely powerful if used correctly. They protect larger pieces, they can block opponents' movements, and they are perfect decoys. Sometimes I will purposely leave one unprotected in order to lure my opponent into thinking I have made a mistake. Through misdirection, you are able to control your rivals' moves and expose any weaknesses they may have.

In order to come out ahead, you always have to understand your opponents' level of ability. If they are unskilled, then you may put in less effort or may take more risks so that you may win quickly. If they are experts, then you have to be more careful and pay attention to the whole board: When they make a move, are they setting you up, or are they falling into your trap? Do they have some ability or talent that you can learn from to improve your game? As you learn to play more and more successfully, you begin to understand yourself and develop your brain for deep thinking.

This is why hobbies are more than just playing around. Life is going to constantly challenge you. You will acquire a set number of skills and attributes that you must learn to use in unison to achieve your goals. Whether you're playing sports, applying for a job, or trying to attract people to you, you are always in competition. And if you are applying for a loan, buying a car or house, or shopping online, your business is the "reward" that others are competing to receive. Understanding how to devise strategies that will accomplish objectives will help you to plan better. Knowing how risk-adverse you are will give you confidence in how far you can go in negotiating, and knowing how comfortable you are in fighting back from adversity will allow you to decide whether you can stay in a bad situation or if you should seek alternate routes.

Hobbies can also help you make connections with others. As I mentioned earlier, one of my favorite hobbies is hiking. I began to walk on hiking trails after I quit smoking in order to start the process of getting back into shape. Hiking brought back memories of being young and exploring the woods in my backyard. As my fitness improved, I began to explore trails that went deeper into the preserve. The more remote the trails, the better opportunities I had to spot deer, turkeys, owls, and other animals. I took pictures and posted them on my Facebook page. This caused others to comment on my posts. On some occasions, I would hike with friends or family members. One year my girlfriend bought me a book on plant species, and I brought the book with me and tried to identify each flower I saw. I hope one day to take a class on herbalism and to learn which plants are edible, which are medicinal, and which are poisonous.

People often say, "If you do what you love for a living, you will never work a day in your life." I have had jobs that I have loved, and I have had jobs that I have hated. It really is a big difference. Don't be afraid to pursue your first love. As I stated earlier, I went to California with a dream of making it as a songwriter; though I didn't succeed, I will never regret trying. If you're interested in learning what makes electrical or mechanical devices work, become an engineer. If you're an artist, you can become a painter, graphic designer, or interior decorator. If you love animals, you can become a vet, wildlife conservation officer, or pet store owner. If you are social, then you can get into a lucrative career selling high-end products or running a company's social media campaign. If you have an interest in a certain career and aren't sure where to begin, start by doing some research. You could network and find people who work in the field and ask them how they got into the profession. Looking for a degree program in your chosen field can give you a taste so that you may see if have the desire or aptitude for the job. Most programs also offer internships, which are a great way to get your foot in the door.

Below is a table to help you choose what you should do in life.

Ability	Jobs to consider
If you are creative	Writer, artist, manager, landscaper/builder
If you enjoy math	Teacher, accountant, engineer, finance
If you enjoy learning/teaching	College professor, trainer, scientist, motivational speaker
If you are athletic	Personal trainer, sports, military/law enforcement
If you are artistic	Marketing professional, artist, musician, interior designer
If you like to bake/cook	Chef, baker, restaurateur, food vendor owner
If you like animals	biologist, veterinarian, conservationist, environmentalist
If you like science	Chemist, astronomer, medical researcher, electrician
If you are social	Hospitality, sales, health-care professional

Hobbies can also help you save money. If you become an expert gardener, for example, you can grow your own produce. This simultaneously increases your consumption of healthy foods, while lowering your grocery bill. Couponing (another hobby) can also help you find deals on everyday products you use. And if you like to work on cars, you'll save on expensive repairs and oil changes by doing the work yourself, and you could use your skills to do work for others and make some extra income on the side. If you are into knitting, woodworking, or making crafts, you could give high-quality presents that you've made yourself for birthdays and holidays, which people always appreciate.

Not all hobbies have to lead you toward making a change, sharpening your mental/physical skills, or increasing your wealth. Some of the best hobbies are those that allow you to simply zone out and relax. These can include listening to music, coloring in books, meditating, or even watching movies. You may like to sleep late, get up and sit on the porch, and read a book. Sometimes we need to take a break and alleviate ourselves from deep thought or worry. If your hobby is having the opposite effects on you, then you need to pick something different to do. For example, you may join a Friday night poker group. You might find yourself drinking more than you should or maybe they gamble a bit and you're losing more money than you can afford. Or, maybe you found an online game that you like and now you are spending too much time on it and it's affecting your schoolwork. The goal is to decrease your level of stress so that you can feel more harmonious.

It's important at this point to address pet ownership. Pets are wonderful additions to your family. They love you unconditionally and are great companions. Too many people get pets that they don't have the time or money to care for, however, either because they didn't realize how much work they would be, or they simply learned that they weren't pet people. Don't get an animal just to draw attention to yourself. Animals are living beings, and they need as much love, attention, and care as any person does. Don't get a pet because you think it will make you cool or because everyone else is doing it. Most animals live for a long time, so there is a huge commitment with adopting a pet; they become attached to their owners, and abandoning a pet can be traumatizing for them. Animals have personalities, just like people do. Some are happy, some are cranky, and some are lazy. Some pets are intelligent, and some are a little less so. Some are social and love to be around people, while some identify with one person only. They can be expensive. If you are struggling to pay your bills, you may not be able to afford the vet bills, special diets, and town licensing fees that comes with owning a pet. If you are juggling multiple jobs or responsibilities, leaving your animal alone for long periods of time may result in you having to constantly to clean up after your pet or repair the damage that it has done to your home. If you do not feel confident that you can provide significant time and money, or if you feel that you will not be a good companion to an animal, please refrain from pet ownership.

CHAPTER 9

LEGACY

THE FINAL ASPECT in building a beautiful life is planning your legacy. What are you about? What do you want to leave behind? These are important questions to consider. Building your legacy helps you pull all these influences together and helps you remain a well-rounded individual. To achieve any level of greatness, you have to build a collection of memories and take advantage of most of your opportunities. You have to have strong, meaningful relationships and live a long, healthy life. You have to have something to leave behind that others can learn from or appreciate. By considering these factors, you have every chance to accomplish all this and more, and leave the legacy that sums up who you are.

What would you most like to change if you could? I have read about species extinction, habitat destruction, and ocean and air pollution, and when I go to the supermarket, I wonder why people are still buying bottled water and using plastic bags. This is something I am passionate about, and I have taken it upon myself to do my share. I use reusable water bottles, I bring reusable bags into stores, I recycle as much as I can in my home, I pick up trash when I'm hiking, and I bought a piece of land that I intend never to develop.

A legacy is more than just being rich and swimming in a pile of cash. It means affecting the world in a positive way and influencing change that will leave the world a little better for the next generation. My cousin coaches kids' soccer and helps children with disabilities. Giving back to your community helps give you a sense of purpose and belonging; it helps you discover and develop skills in a way that is not otherwise possible. It makes you humble, and makes you realize that there is more to the world than your goals, your accomplishments, and your fears. We live in a world that is rife with insecurity, violence, fear, and selfishness, and people are becoming desensitized to it all. While it is important as you find success to remember where you came from and how you got there, it is also important to realize what you have learned, and what you can give back.

People are sometimes afraid to be creative and to question the status quo. The beauty of having independent thought is to be able to look around us and either make what we see better, or change the things we think are wrong. I have written songs for most of my life, and people often tell me that they wish they could do that, too. I always tell them that they can, and they give me a disapproving look and restate the fact that they can't. They can't, because they have given up before they even try. Yes, to some extent, some people are more creative and talented than others. I am far from being a great guitar player, but I was able to hone my craft by committing myself to practicing for hours every day when I was younger. I still make sure I pick up the guitar at least once a week to keep up with it. As with most skills, the instant you stop using them, you lose them. On the other hand, I would love to learn how to paint or speak another language. I took a painting class in high school, and though learning techniques helped improve my product, I don't have the knack for it to be a world-famous artist—but I know I can still use art as a creative outlet if I so choose. The same goes for learning a foreign language. I always wanted be able to speak Spanish. I took classes in high school and college, but I realized that the way to become fluent is to be in an environment where you use it regularly.

The point is that you can improve your ability in any skill that you actually put the time and effort into developing. There are millions of opportunities to develop or improve your skills. Local colleges offer courses, and some towns offer night classes to residents. You can learn things from pottery to gardening at a local level, and they are generally lower in cost. All you need is to have the desire to find and attend the programs.

Creativity will move you beyond simply being able to create a piece of artwork or a poem. Creativity can assist you in all forms and mediums in your life. The basis of creativity is being able to find something in a space where nothing exists. You could be faced with a new problem at work that no one had encountered before: if you are a creative thinker, you could find and present a solution and be the hero. The more you believe in your ability to solve problems, the more the skill will develop. This is the one skill I am most proud to possess. It is a rare occurrence when someone comes to me with an issue, or when I am struggling to accomplish something, and I can't stop and take a couple of seconds and think of a way or two to solve the problem. Being a great problem solver will make you the one coworkers come to. This helps you stand out from the crowd and will be sure to lead to greater opportunities in the workplace.

Creative people also develop a stronger sense of creativity, because the more they see solutions, the more they want to find even better ones. They start spending more time analyzing and breaking things down, and begin to create deeper thinking and stronger mental maps. This is where people find love in learning and pride in their accomplishments. I can't overstate how important a tool this is.

Besides creativity, do not be afraid to take a stand. Fight for what is right. Search for change when you see people continuing to do the wrong things. This is difficult to do; for the most part, people allow themselves to be led like sheep. They fear that if they speak up, they will be put down, ignored, or thought of negatively by others. They don't want to rock the boat. The greatest societies were built by people who did rock the boat (so to speak), and those are the people who are most remembered in history—for good or bad. You cannot hide behind fear and let things continue to happen that you know are wrong. This holds true with your political views. If you are unhappy with your town's ordinances, zoning rules, or taxes, you can do something about it. First, you can talk to your town leaders. If you can't get the answers you're looking for, then maybe you can run for the town council or the zoning board.

Even if you don't get the position, you could still make valuable connections and learn about the processes that are required to run the local government effectively.

If you don't want to take it that far, then you might consider donating your time to a political chapter and thereby help a candidate get elected. Find out who is running for office and what platforms the nominee stands on. It's hard to get everything you want out of political candidates: they have to make decisions that they feel are best for all of their constituents, and not just a few. You also have to realize that senators and representatives are part of a minority or a majority. If the political party that is in control favors raising taxes and spending, then you may not get as much of an income tax return as you may be accustomed to; on the other hand, if you hoped that a local farm would get preserved, that same party may be more open to supporting legislation to help make that happen.

No matter which way you lean, be careful with how you choose your politics. Make sure that you aren't choosing a side because your friends, family, or teachers try to convince you to do so. Take time to research the stance of all of the candidates—what they are for, what they are against—and pick values that they have in common with your own. Failing to do so could leave you supporting candidates who directly conflict with your core principles.

Don't be afraid to stand up for what you believe in. I know we cannot all be great leaders. Not everyone is an Abraham Lincoln or a Warren Buffett or a Steve Jobs, but we *can* be more than mere passengers on a bus to nowhere. If you are unhappy with what you see around you, then you have to be the lightning rod of change; you have to set the example. Whether it is educating someone, supporting a cause that others reject, or simply lending a hand to those in need, you cannot live in fear that your actions will turn people off. If you have strong convictions and build the right kinds of relationships, then you should have the proper support to back your decisions. People who let fear control them will never realize their full potential: they will veer off at the first sign of resistance. People—including your own family—will try to discourage you because they don't want to see you succeed where they have failed. But when we finally overcome our adversity in life, we can look back and appreciate how large the mountain was that we climbed to get there: how strong our resolve was, and how brave we were when facing our challenges. That's when the path we have left behind for others to follow becomes clear and visible.

You also have to think about your family—including your children, nieces, nephews, cousins, and so on. This is especially true in families that are stuck in poverty, or where family members battle addictions or mental illness (or a combination of these factors). If you grow up in one of these households and are the one who is breaking the cycle, then it is your obligation to try to help the younger members of your family see the light. While you may well disagree with me, someone has to lead the way. Older generations of your family may not have figured out how to break out of poverty or deal with depression, and may be sowing these seeds of unhealthy habits upon the younger members of the family. If these people are their only role models, then they will grow up with the impression that things are hopeless and that there is nothing they can ever do to succeed. The parents may not have the skills to teach their children how to learn and how to avoid peer pressure, or about the risks of drinking alcohol and doing drugs. Poverty is tough to overcome, but it is a choice. The United States was built by poor immigrants who only had a dream and a desire to be more than they were: anyone who wants to succeed here simply has to get his or her priorities in order and learn how to get on the right track.

You may doubt that it's as easy as that. Well yes, it is. It all starts with setting goals. You can only change your life by taking one step at a time. As the saying says, "Rome wasn't built in a day." There is no miracle potion for success. Some are blessed with greatness and fail, and some are born into failure yet still manage to succeed. You can start by setting small, simple goals that you want to accomplish. You can say, "This semester, I want to raise my GPA from 3.0 to 3.2," "I want to save a hundred dollars this month," or "I want to exercise five days a week and lose a couple of pounds." Setting goals is easy. Pick out something you want to improve, and improve it.

How will losing a couple of pounds or getting a higher grade in class help you in the long run? As you accomplish your minor goals, you can start to set larger goals. You can set short-term and long-term goals, and you can set personal and financial goals. The more you accomplish, the more your self-esteem will increase, and the more you will know that you are capable of doing anything you put your mind to. That's the point: you don't know what you can do until you try it, and you can't know where to start if you don't allow yourself to have any vision. If you want to make money through renting properties, but you don't have much money, then how can this work? You start by buying one property and fixing it up, and then you save up and buy a second property and rent out the first, and so on until eventually you will become a real-estate mogul.

You can't predict unknown factors. The first house could be a money pit, you could lose your job, or the market could crash, but if you never try to pursue your goals, then you will never know what could have been. Looking back, you don't want to be thinking, "I could have done this," or "I could have done that." From a young age, you have to develop a mind-set that you will be faced with many possibilities along the way, and that not all of them will work out. If you don't give up, there will always be another opportunity. If you want to own a landscaping company, for instance, buy a used lawnmower and start going door to door so that you can pick up a few accounts. As you make money, you can buy more tools and offer more and more services. As your clientele notices your good work and starts to spread your name around, you will pick up more customers. Soon enough, you'll have to hire a couple of people to keep up with the increased demand. One day you may reach the point where you will need to buy a building for your business and begin to advertise to attract larger clients. While this won't always be the case, it is certainly possible. Believe in yourself, and give yourself the opportunity to prove what you *can* do, instead of dwelling on what you *cannot* do.

I was always creative and always had the desire to write. My legacy is this book. It is the sum of all that I have learned through my struggles in life. My goal is to share my wisdom and experiences so that others can avoid the pitfalls or indecisions that I have struggled with throughout most of my life. Too often have I watched people struggle, and only as they age do they come to understand that they could have done things differently. I am one of those people, and it is my personal mission to reach as many people as I can and to get them to realize that there is always hope, there is always opportunity, and there can always be forgiveness. Wanting success does not entitle you to it: there has to be a little bit of sense and a whole lot of effort to make it happen.

CONCLUSION

I KNOW MY thoughts may appear to repeat or jump around from subject to subject, but my goal in this book is to show you how many different factors in life are actually interrelated. Making one good decision can lead to a whole host of good decisions; conversely, one bad decision can lead you to make other bad choices.

To summarize the important points in these chapters, first you need to take care of your health, both mentally and physically. Not only are they intertwined, but they will contribute to your inner strength. You need to learn to take care of yourself, appreciate yourself, and protect yourself from all the things in life that will try to test you. Having a strong mental and physical core will give you the confidence to set yourself up for success and to endure all the challenges life will throw at you.

Once you have a strong base, you need to surround yourself with the best people possible. These are people who love you unconditionally, will do anything they can to help you, and who have the right attitudes and abilities to help you grow—and vice versa. Engaging in unhealthy relationships will hold you back and will prevent you from reaching the high levels of happiness that you deserve.

With a proper supporting cast around you and a winning attitude, it's time to determine what profession you are interested in pursuing and provide yourself with an education that will put you on the right path to success. Focus on the career that will reward you both mentally and financially. Money isn't everything, so doing what you love is the more important factor here. And even when you *are* heading in the right direction, keep on learning: this will help shape you into a well-rounded person, it gives you opportunities to discover new interests or hobbies, and it helps protect you in case you find yourself in a dying trade or a stagnant company. Educating yourself will also help you find opportunities to grow financially, professionally, and personally.

After you have secured stable employment, look for ways to build your money. Remember the saying, "Money makes money." The more money you have, the more opportunities you will have to increase your worth. People often tell me, "I have too many bills," or "I don't make enough." These are valid points, but there is always room to save. You may need to sacrifice a comfort or two—those things that you want more than actually need. If you can, save or invest at least in the range of 15 to 20 percent of your earnings. The younger you start doing this, the more it will become a habit, and you will be able to adjust to spending less money over time. Proper saving can help you purchase a nice home, a reliable car, and give you a good start to raising a family. This will also set you up for a comfortable retirement in which you won't have to struggle to survive during your older years.

If you can accomplish all of this, then you can work on building a legacy: you can leave something behind for others to benefit from. This could be setting aside money for a scholarship, starting a research foundation, or donating a piece of land for preservation. You could leave college money for your kids or grandkids. If you want to go into politics, you could create a piece of legislation that is dear to your heart. You could start a family business to pass down to your children. You could write a book, paint a masterpiece, or craft a beautiful table and chairs that can be handed down generation to generation. Your legacy will outlast you and will be appreciated by future generations. It can be teaching something to your children. I developed a lot of who I am because I idolized my grandfather. I wanted to be like him, and, though we had different personalities, I borrowed several attributes from him that I was able to implement into who I am. Sometimes I do things and I think, "Yup! That's what Gramps would have done!" That is his legacy. This is something personal that you will have to discover for yourself and to work toward.

While all of this seems simple, we are not all cut from the same cloth. Some of us are born into poverty. Some of us were raised in households of violence and abuse or drug use. Or perhaps we were born into wonderful homes, but we simply made a few bad decisions that now make it difficult for us to get ahead; or maybe we are shy and we just don't have the confidence to try to reach our goals; and so on.

Keep in mind that you cannot compare yourself to others or to other people's accomplishments or failures. You have to follow your own path and believe in yourself. All of the tools I have listed in this book are suggestions for beginning to build (or, if necessary, rebuilding) your future. You will not be able to accomplish all of your goals all at once, and you cannot change your whole life overnight. But you can outline a step-by-step plan that is best suited for you; you will slowly start to make progress when you stick with this plan. The remainder of this book will help you do just that.

If this is where you find yourself and you are ready to make these changes, realize that people who are struggling around you may hope that you fail: they may not be as strong as you are and have difficulty watching you pull yourself out of the hole that you may be in. It may be hard for them to see you succeed and know that they could do the same, if only they had the ability or the drive to do so. They may try to belittle your accomplishments and make you feel like you are acting like you are superior to them. Or it may strain a relationship because you no longer have much in common. You can't allow these people to hold you back, because they might just be doing that out of a combination of fear and jealousy (unless you are turning into a jerk; if you are, then you need to reevaluate yourself and your situation).

Don't be afraid to seek help through professional counselors: not only for career or financial advice, but also in helping you overcome any mental or physical condition that you may have. There is no shame in admitting that you cannot deal with an issue alone. If you are holding yourself back because of something that happened in the past, then it will be hard for you to succeed in the future. And don't be afraid to learn from those who have been there and have overcome things themselves; they have blazed the trail. They know the obstacles you face, and they may be willing to share their ideas to help you head in the right direction.

Also realize that you will find success in some things and you may not in others. You may be great at finding the right kind of relationship, but fail at managing your money correctly. Cherish what you do well, and work on the things that are more challenging for you. We can never be perfect, but there is no reason that we cannot work toward achieving excellence in all phases of our lives.

Most important, do not allow fear to control you. Overcome your insecurities and shortcomings. Look at yourself honestly and identify your weaknesses, and work on them so that they don't hurt you over the long term. You cannot be afraid to try to accomplish things that seem impossible, and you should never settle for what you know is beneath what you deserve. You can only do this by developing your toolbox of skills, abilities, attributes, and experiences. Understand how you can combine being strong both mentally and physically, gaining an education, getting the right job, finding the right friends, and picking the right person to spend your life with, and how all of these things can affect every single thing you do in life. Even if you don't become the president of the United States, you could be a state senator. Even if you cannot be an astronaut, you can still work for NASA. Perhaps you wish you could be a famous painter, but you cannot paint; you could still work for a museum. The only way you can truly and completely fail in life is to not try at all.

SWOT ANALYSIS AND BUILDING YOUR TOOLBOX

YOU CAN TALK all you want about improving or changing the direction of your life, but to increase your chance of success, I advise that you do some soul searching and start a personal ability toolbox. Maximizing your tools, such as skills, your attributes, and abilities, will have a major impact on you throughout your life. In order to figure out where you are in life, begin with a "SWOT" analysis. This is a term used in the business world to identify *S*trengths, *W*eaknesses, *O*pportunities, and *T*hreats when doing strategic planning. These are composed of internal and external factors that could help you succeed or limit your options. Your strengths will be the things you do well; perhaps you have a set of skills or a specific attribute that is very desirable. Weaknesses are the things you don't do well; for me this is public speaking, but for you they might include any physical or mental attributes that make it harder for you to reach your goals. Opportunities are paths or occurrences that can propel you forward, such as going to college or accepting a new position at work that has more room for growth. Threats are factors that may disrupt your goals. If you are training to become a travel agent, for instance, that may not be a great idea, since that trade has mostly been replaced by various online tools and the prevalence of social media. If the housing market is bad, it may not be a time to get into real estate. This list will vary from person to person. If you have difficulty coming up with your own personal factors, then ask close friends or family members to assist. This isn't a matter of ego; it's simply a matter of creating a realistic view of yourself so that you can analyze where you are in life and what things you need to work on in order to take better advantage of your talents.

To make this clearer, I will demonstrate a SWOT analysis for me writing this book. My *strengths* are that I'm creative and determined, I've gained a lot of knowledge in overcoming my own personal barriers, and I've always had a knack for expressing myself in my writings. My *weaknesses* include my fear of public speaking, and the fact that I can be reclusive and that sometimes I need to be prodded and exposed to new things before I will feel comfortable trying them on my own. My *opportunities* are that there is a need out there in the world for the information I have collected and shared, and that discovering self-publishing has given me the ability to get my material out there. If I am successful, I could turn to writing as a career, since I've already finished a novel and am working on a second. My *threats* are that I may be perceived as lacking sufficient credentials to write a self-help book (I do not have a social science degree, nor does my profession directly correlate to writing this type of material). Publishing this book also does not guarantee me any success, and I could end up losing money and the time I put into the realization of this goal.

These positive and negative factors have given me a lot to think about. While the negative aspects do concern me, I'm confident that the strength of the material I've written and my accomplishments in greatly improving my own situation in life will more than make up for my lack of perceived qualifications. My eagerness to learn and challenge myself will help me to thwart my fears of failure. My interest in these topics and the love of sharing knowledge will make me the perfect pitchman. And the publishing of this book allows me a platform for sharing my writings with others, which for me is a huge sign of success, no matter what the outcome.

You can use this SWOT analysis for just about any decision you want to make, whether it be deciding what college to attend, what city to live in, whether you should change your job, or whether you should buy a home or if you should rent. Your SWOT analysis can be simple or complex. The more information you obtain, the easier it will be to make a prudent decision. Now that you have (I hope) done some self-evaluation and have set forth a few ideas to explore, we can take a deeper look into understanding the power of your personality.

In this next part of the book, I list several key attributes for you to consider working on in order to build your own toolbox that can help you realize your goals. Then I will share a few insights into common fears that can cause people to give up too quickly. I want to assure you that everyone faces adversity, and I'll show you how to avoid feeling trapped by it. Next, I want to address behaviors that could cause bumps in your path to success. Sometimes we get too comfortable and set in our ways and begin to develop bad habits that may end up hurting us. If you want to continually strive for success, then you have to avoid becoming complacent and accepting where you are in life. You should consistently strive for your personal and professional betterment.

Finally, I'll touch on a few skills that many may see as being undesirable, but that can actually be quite valuable. Since we all come from different places in life, and we are taught to view the world in different ways, I find it difficult for me to judge what is right and what is wrong; I can only give you my own personal views. If you can "hustle," then instead of trying to sell illegal substances, try your hand at selling houses or cars. If people find you to be loud and annoying, then find a job being a radio announcer or a docent at a museum.

TOOLBOX

Your toolbox contains your strengths and guides you toward making better decisions. Because these skills seem basic and simple enough, it is easy to overlook them and to lull ourselves into being satisfied in our current situations. It is rare for someone to master all of these tools, but the more of them you can work on obtaining, the better your chances for success. For example, I have an amazing ability to self-reflect and easily adapt, but I am constantly working on my ability to communicate with others, and I could do a far better job of being patient. You should be able to openly praise yourself for having strong skills, and to openly criticize yourself for things you can improve on. I am constantly trying to be more patient and to communicate more effectively. At the same time, I am still finding new ways to self-analyze and increase my basis of knowledge so that I can adapt more easily. By improving my communication, patience, adaptability, and self-reflecting skills, I am also learning how to be more diplomatic and improving my situational awareness. The more you hone your abilities, the more extensive they will become. Only by knowing and improving on who you are can you work at becoming the person you hope to be.

ABILITY TO REFLECT/SELF-REFLECT

The more you can reflect on your actions and surroundings, the more you will understand the cause-and-effect relationships of your decisions. The less mystery in life, the easier it becomes to maneuver into positive positions. You can confidently appraise what you do well and what you need to work on. Knowing who you are and what you are capable of will guide you to pursue opportunities that fall within your strengths, and it will help you avoid getting hindered by your weaknesses. Understanding yourself also allows you to better communicate with people in your personal and/or professional life. The easier it is for you to tell people what you like and what you dislike, the less room there will be for misunderstandings. You may not like a particular task in a job you are applying for; if your dislike of that task outweighs the positives, then it may be best to forego that opportunity.

Finally, those who self-reflect will have a clearer picture of why things happen in their personal or professional relationships. Perhaps you weren't chose for a project for a legitimate reason: it could have been that another team member had stronger skills that were an overriding need for that project. Having this skill helps you avoid making snap judgments and creating controversy because of a perceived slight.

ABILITY TO REFLECT ON OTHERS

Everyone has a set of skills or abilities that differentiates one person from another. One person may be a slow learner but is charismatic, while another person may be good at math, but lacks communication skills. It is important to be able to identify and realize the different things that people can bring to you, and you to them. Just as you do with yourself, learn how to identify others' strengths and weaknesses. Failure to do this may cause you to reject people who might otherwise play major roles in your future successes. As with assembling a puzzle, it is not always clear where every piece will fit, but without all the pieces, you won't get a clear picture. Don't undervalue people, as everyone has a purpose.

There is great strength in being able to reflect on why other people exhibit different behaviors from you. Understanding why they act in certain ways can lead you to identify characteristics that may help you improve the relationship, or to help others who cannot see the reasons for people's actions to be more empathetic. If a close friend has a promising chance of getting a scholarship for playing sports, but is having trouble in math (which you happen to excel in), you can offer tutoring and give your friend a chance to achieve success. Your friend may be too proud or stubborn to ask for help, in which case he or she would lose out on a big opportunity. Awareness of why the people in your environment act certain ways will help you navigate and make better decisions about what you are doing, which people you should surround yourself with, and what you'll get out of being a part of a particular group.

ABILITY TO COMMUNICATE

The easier it is for people to understand you, the more harmonious relationships will be. A huge problem in many relationships is the inability to properly communicate with one another, which can lead to major disconnections. This can hurt you both personally and professionally. Communicating effectively demonstrates intelligence and the ability to convey your message. When you do this, people will feel that you are listening to their concerns and that you are relaying your understanding. You might share with them the insights that were instrumental in forming the basis of your opinion, which could help to sway them to your side.

ABILITY TO MEDIATE

It's hard to not take sides when you're surrounded by conflict: you generally want to support your friend, a colleague you work well with, or a process you believe in, or you may dislike the person or process that is the cause of the conflict. Someone who has the ability to see both sides and to give an honest account of the situation is both rare and valuable. If you can give fair points to both sides and help others reach a compromise, then you could help defuse tension, improve practices, and demonstrate that you have leadership abilities.

The trick is to be able to isolate yourself from the issue or the people attached and examine the situation using a SWOT analysis. Once you list positive and negative factors and decide what you would do in the situation, you can develop the best possible outcome. You can then explain how you came up with the conclusion using the positive and negative factors from each side. If the subject is too personal for you to be properly objective, then may have to be honest and work with someone who is not as involved in order to come up with a fair compromise. Your goal is to create positive relationships and to solve problems in a positive manner.

ABILITY TO LISTEN

Listening is a fundamental tool in relationship building and planning, and in recognizing what people are looking for from you. People with vast amounts of knowledge are generally eager to impart what they know if you give them a chance. Seek these people out and engage them in your common interests. You will be amazed at how much good information they will share with you and help you to see things from a new perspective. The knowledge you gain could cause you to revise what you previously thought was the right thing to do. Second, the more you listen, the more you will learn. Most goals that you set are generally best met with a plan: the more information you collect, the easier it will become to map out the steps you need to take to accomplish those goals. Finally, sometimes people have trouble understanding what others want from them. If you take time to listen to what people are telling you, you may see subtle hints that you didn't recognize before. Someone may be joking that you need to be nicer to customers in the workplace. Even though the person may appear to be joking, it could be obvious to everyone else that this really is a problem that could threaten your employment. It's wise to know what people expect from you, get an idea of what they currently think of you, and determine what attributes you can improve on if needed.

In any relationship, listening is the key to success. Again, subtle hints from a friend or partner can be indicators of discord, and if you don't pick up on them, you could risk losing a relationship that is important to you. It's easy to get caught up inside of ourselves because we can't visually see how other people think; we can only get a feeling or try to communicate with words. If you are not a good listener, then you should work on this skill immediately. Although you may not be as empathetic as others, with work, you can increase your awareness of others and how they feel.

ABILITY TO ADAPT

Adaptability is important in the modern world. Things constantly change, including technology, laws, the economy, job locations, and people. It's easy to get left behind if you don't keep up with current trends or if you aren't able to change with the times. This can be as simple as being open to a new operating system at work, choosing to pursue a degree in an emerging technology, or volunteering to attend a conference to learn more about the industry you are in. Due to uncertainty caused by an ever-changing business landscape, it's important to make learning a lifelong goal; to form meaningful, resilient relationships; and to not become too accustomed to a high level of wealth, because your life could change without warning.

You may need to change professions. Employers are attracted to diverse candidates who can handle multiple roles and fit in wherever a need appears. Being adaptable will help you build job security and will make you a valuable contributor to whatever group or organization you belong to. It will also give you confidence if you end up out of work and have to settle for a job that is beneath previous paygrade. You can settle for the lower paying job, knowing you have the skills to climb the ladder.

Finally, proper money management will help you endure transitions. If you overleverage your finances, and a moment arises where your income is interrupted, you risk losing valuable assets. If you manage your money correctly, your greatest risk will be depleting your reserves: you can always make more money, but it is hard to regain the value from having to sell off collectables, property, or even stocks. You put so much time, effort, and research into acquiring your wealth; the last thing you want to do is lose it.

ABILITY TO FORGIVE

Though people and/or situations can hurt us, we must not forget how to forgive. If we are unable to forgive, then we hold something negative close to our hearts. While this motivates some, it generally destroys those who are overconsumed with hate, regret, or sadness. People are not perfect, and we all make mistakes—some more than others, and some more intentionally than others. You don't have to forget, and it's more than acceptable to feel hurt, but there will come a time when you will have to look past the transgression and move on. Those who hold on to the past will be left behind.

ABILITY TO BE SITUATIONALLY AWARE

You have to fully understand the situations you are in if you want to make the best judgments. Sometimes you have to make quick decisions with little information, and you can only make the decision you feel is best at the time. At other times, in contrast, you may have more time to prepare. While this is a general statement, one factor that can help is to develop a feeling for how people think. You can do this by listening to what they say, recognizing patterns, trusting your gut, and asking questions to see how they respond. Be aware of your environment. Looking around the office during an interview may give you an idea of the values of the person who is interviewing you. Or perhaps you are going out with a friend and visiting someone you don't know: be aware of the location and the things you see around you. Know the people you can go to when you have a problem or an issue that you don't have a strong understanding about. If you are having car problems, for instance, seek a close friend who knows cars; before making a major financial move, talk with someone who is successful with money; and so on. In the workplace, do the things that are expected of you, but find out where there are opportunities for you to shine, and take hold of them. Understand when you are caught in a bad situation and find a way to minimize the damage— or remove yourself entirely. Get a feeling for what people expect from you and what they think you are capable of. Most importantly, learn to know when to use that situation to your advantage and when to come clean and be honest.

ABILITY TO BE CONFIDENT

Trust in yourself, and market your abilities. People want to be surrounded by others who believe in themselves and can help lead them to success. Those who are unsure and frightened will turn others off, and those people will look elsewhere for leadership or direction. If you seem to be shy or quiet when you are applying for a job, you may appear to be uninterested in the opportunity; the hiring manager may think you are unmotivated and unprepared and, ultimately, may decide that you are not the best candidate for the job. Potential mates are looking for people who know who they are and where they want to go in life. If you want to land the best partner, you have to be prepared to show that you have solid goals and visions for your shared future.

ABILITY TO LEARN

We live in an ever-changing world, and the instant you learn something, something new that you don't know will replace it. College will give you skills and prepare you for your chosen career path, but you also learn how to learn and how to work with other people. All the courses you take will help you build connections from one subject to the next. You will learn how math is related to statistics, which is related to economics, which is related to the stock market, which is related to ethics, which is related to social problems, which is related to the environment, and so on. You learn how to tackle problems that you wouldn't have known where to begin with in the past. You'll be required to work in groups, and you'll see that while some people work well in teams, others do not. You'll get to explore subjects you wouldn't have thought you were interested in, such as art, music, history, and science. The more you understand the dynamic connections of everything in life, the less complicated everything seems, even as you learn that there is always more to learn. You feel like you could learn to understand almost anything. This is important, because to be truly successful and/or fulfilled, most people will have to keep learning for the rest of their lives. If we want to stay relevant, we must embrace technology as it changes and stay in the forefront; we have to understand where the world is going, and make sure that we stay onboard.

ABILITY TO BUILD RELATIONSHIPS
This goes beyond the ability to network. Relationship building is the ability to figure out who to surround yourself with and who not to. This is what I meant earlier in the book when I discussed finding people with common goals whom you can work with to help elevate one another to higher levels. Whether it is friends, colleagues, other students, or potential dating partners, understanding the right people to build relationships with can bring you not only more success but, ultimately, more happiness.

ABILITY TO BE PASSIONATE
Those who are passionate are able to inspire others. Passionate people truly love what they are doing and genuinely care about others. When you have passion, it forces people to look and see what you are seeing,

because—let's face it—most people want to reach that same level of satis-faction and struggle to do so. Finding something that you have so much love for is a gift, and you should cherish that gift and learn how to share it with others. Passionate people work hard to solve problems, recruit others, and create a warm environment that is conducive to learning and sharing knowledge.

ABILITY TO BUILD YOUR SKILLS

This goes without saying. The more you know how to do, the more valu-able you will be to others and to yourself. Learn to be a jack-of-all-trades who knows a little bit about everything. Not only will this help you inter-act with others, but it will mean that you will always have a basic under-standing of any issues you may encounter. You may not be a great auto mechanic, for instance, but maybe you can learn enough to do basic maintenance on your car. The more you understand about plumbing and carpentry, the more you will save on home repairs. Understand financial basics so that you can get better loans, invest your money more wisely, and get more money back in taxes. Learn how to build a fire, navigate by the sun, or grow your own food. I could list countless things here, but the point is that the more you know, the more interesting you will become, and the more advantages you will have in life.

ABILITY TO BE PROACTIVE

You should strive to be *proactive* rather than *reactive*. Those who are pro-active see the challenges that are coming in the future, instead of being surprised by them in the present. When you have a car, for instance, if you keep up on the maintenance and get regular oil changes, it will last longer. If you neglect to do these things and the car breaks down on you on your way to work, you will not only have to pay more for repairs—because a new engine costs a lot more than an oil change—but it will also cost you valuable time and will be a major inconvenience. This also goes for schoolwork, household chores, and tasks at work. The more ahead of things you are, the more time you will have to relax and do the things you want to do. You will not be afraid of challenges, because you will develop the skills of providing resolutions to problems and identifying issues before they become problems in the first place. Another example is that you don't know how long a paper will take to write, but if you wait until the last minute to get started, you may find yourself handing in subpar work, and your grade will suffer. This is not a matter of being a show-off; instead, it is a matter of understanding ways to make your future easier by tackling small challenges before they are allowed to metastasize into something that is harder to resolve.

Some people excel under pressure and do great work the closer they get to a deadline. I can understand that thought process, but the more responsibilities you have to do all at once, the more difficult and stressful it becomes to juggle multiple tasks. If you like to write papers at the last minute, look at what other tasks you can accomplish ahead of time so that you will have the time to do the best job possible on your report.

ABILITY TO TAKE OWNERSHIP/ACCOUNTABILITY/RESPONSIBILITY

Taking *ownership* of a task or situation shows that you take the work personally: you truly care if you succeed or fail. Taking *accountability* shows that you are willing to take the repercussions for failure, but it also means that you get the glory if all goes well. When you show that you are willing to risk your reputation, it helps build your character and also shows others that you are not afraid to take on bigger tasks. Having *responsibility* means that you will do whatever it takes to accomplish the task, whether it is working harder, helping others, or putting in more time. This also shows people that they can count on you in tough situations and that you are a desirable addition to the team in a crunch. All three of these attributes will work for you in return. The more you feel obligated to accomplish something, the harder you will push yourself; the harder you push yourself, the more situations you will put yourself in. And the more situations you put yourself in, the more you will be able to network, learn to solve problems, and obtain new knowledge and skills.

ABILITY TO HAVE HOBBIES

Be well rounded. Understand the importance of play, rest, and relaxation, and know how to recharge your batteries. Having a hobby truly is an ability; it gives you something to help offset the stress of work or home life, and it gives you something to look forward to when you have free time. Hobbies help you connect with other individuals, and they give you something to talk about with new acquaintances. Hobbies can bring you positive feelings and give you something to lift you up when you feel down. They make you more diverse in the people you know and the activities you engage in, and they help you see things from different angles. For example online games can increase your leadership skills and abilities to work in a team. You may socialize with people who come from different walks in life and create positive, long lasting relationships.

ABILITY TO IMPROVE YOUR DIET

Knowing what you are putting into your body is another important ability. The better you eat, the healthier you will feel. And as you eat foods that offer more nutrition, the less your body will feel the need to consume. There are so many widely available and diverse foods out there today that it should be easy to find healthy items that you will enjoy. As you age, diet becomes increasingly important; as our metabolisms slow down, we no longer burn calories as easily as we did in our youth. If we don't eat right, we face various problems with cholesterol, diabetes, heart disease, and high blood pressure.

ABILITY TO EXERCISE

This is similar to the ability to have a good diet: the more you take care of your body, the healthier and happier you will be in life. As you get older, the less active you become and the quicker your body will break down; and whether we want to accept it or not, the better shape you are in, the more you will attract people. You will also attract the higher end of the spectrum of person you are looking for. This is not simply a matter of judging by appearances, but rather is an indication of a person's overall health. You will seem more motivated, more confident, and fit than people who do not care for themselves. Although we have evolved, we still have the desire to follow the strongest and best-looking people. If you can use this as a personal strength, then do so. Just be sure not to depend solely on this attribute, or to allow it to lead you into make poor decisions about your direction in life.

ABILITY TO BE PATIENT
Success cannot be achieved overnight. You have to carefully plan your path in life, and take things one step at a time. A lot of people give up on their goals because their goals seem too far away to reach. Resist that logic and keep moving toward your goal, step by step. Of course you don't want to move at a snail's pace (if you do, you need to reevaluate your plan). Those who stay true to the course they have set generally reach levels of success that they will find satisfying. Also, don't be afraid to take a step back if it will lead to more opportunity in the long run. This can be a smart move; redirection is sometimes the perfect cure for stagnation. You can also use this strategy in cultivating relationships. By being patient, you show the other person that you are mature and confident. A person who can remain calm and collected gives off a sense of control, which is a highly desirable quality in potential relationship candidates. People who are impatient are sometimes hard to deal with, they often overlook mistakes, they may not perform at expected levels, and they give the impression that other people and their needs are not as important as their own. Although you can try to manage conflicts with impatient people, be aware that doing so may escalate the tension between you.

ABILITY TO HAVE AN EVEN KEEL
Life can sometimes be a bit of a roller coaster of emotions. Whether you're up for a new job, you receive a bill that you can't afford, or you end up with an unexpected sum of money, it's important not to let yourself get overwhelmed by the highs and lows in life. Have some perspective in every challenge and every opportunity that comes up. Allowing yourself

to get too low can cause you to take up unhealthy habits to compensate for your disappointment; these unhealthy habits can then lead you to make bad decisions, which in turn can further compound the challenges you face. On the other hand, if you get too high, you may neglect other options that are available to you; for example, you may become conceited and damage important relationships. Of course, it's good to get excited and it's fine to be disappointed: just remember to stay true to yourself and you will overcome your lows and do the best with your highs.

ABILITY TO MANAGE TIME

Another excellent trait is having the ability to be punctual. Many people struggle with this; they can miss out on valuable opportunities, and may even gain a bad reputation for being unreliable. If you have trouble showing up on time, then I suggest that you should work at being fifteen minutes early to school, work, or any other important engagements. Time management is also the function of learning how to prioritize tasks to efficiently complete projects and/or deadlines on time. This could be as simple as listing the steps you required to successfully complete your assignment, or working on a more difficult task first to prevent you from getting overwhelmed by everything you need to do. The more eager you are to take on a challenge, the easier it will be to complete it. Good time management skills cut down on your stress and improve your confidence. This is another skill that will help you shine in your personal and professional aspirations.

DON'T FEAR

The reason that most people fail is because they are afraid that they are not good enough or don't have the right skills, or they don't know where to start. They may be hesitant, holding on to past failures, which causes them to latch onto anything that seems safe. This book is trying to motivate those who want more than to just accept what they now have and are pushing for a higher level of success. Everyone experiences some form of rejection or failure in life; it is how you handle yourself when things are rough that determines how high you can truly climb.

REJECTION

They say, "If at first you don't succeed, try, try again." Rejection is not always because you are not what someone is looking for or that you are not the best candidate. Sometimes you encounter bad timing, or the potential employer may have someone else in mind or feel you lack experience or give off the wrong vibe. When you are rejected, don't get angry. Evaluate the situation and see what, if anything, you could have done better. If you learn what you can improve, then you will be better prepared for the next situation. If you did everything you could, then you should simply realize that this wasn't your opportunity.

Although I am mainly referring to being a candidate for a job or position, this also translates to relationships. If you are rejected by a person or a group of people, then it only means that they aren't the types of people you want to build relationships with. As I discussed earlier, you want to be with people who are positive and who will help you build up to greater things in life, not those who will drag you down. You want to be with people who are interested in getting to know you and seeing the potential you possess. Time and energy spent either being angry or pursuing those who have rejected you could be better spent on engaging in more constructive plans and actions to improve yourself and in finding those who do share your ideals and values.

FAILURE

As with rejection, sometimes you can overreach and can't handle what you have taken on. Maybe you started a business and found that you did a poor job managing the finances. Or, you got promoted into a leadership role at work, but had trouble motivating people. Learn from your failures. Find ways to shore up the attributes you struggled with, either by furthering your education, finding a mentor, or participating in training programs. If you are still having issues, then you may need to reevaluate your goals.

In relationships, find the common reasons to explain why you are unable to maintain connections with others. Are you continuously dating people who cheat on you? What are some common characteristics of the people you date? If need be, ask some close friends or family members what they think you're doing wrong. I guarantee they'll be happy to provide some insight and thus help prevent you from being hurt again.

By learning from our failures, we can take steps to reduce or avoid failures altogether. This is why they are so important. We cannot learn what we are doing wrong if our mistakes aren't brought to light. But if we are afraid to fail, then we will never know how far we can push ourselves and what we are capable of, and we won't develop the strength to pick ourselves up when we fall.

CREATIVITY

This is my personal favorite attribute. Creativity is what makes being human such a gift. It has a tremendous number of benefits. It makes you a good problem solver, it gives you the desire to grow and explore, it helps you connect with other people because of your ability to share a part of yourself with others, and it helps release stress that might otherwise build up. Some say that you are either born with creativity or you are not, while others say you can develop it. I think it's somewhere in the middle. Some people are obviously born with a strong creative ability, but I also believe that if you desire to be creative, you can hone this skill.

To be a creative problem solver, look at issues from all sides. Someone says minimum wage is good, for example, and you disagree. Look at the benefits for those who make minimum wage. Will it help reduce poverty? Does it affect a large percentage of the population? Will it improve the economy? Then ask questions of its negative impacts. Will it hurt small business owners? Will they hire fewer people? Will raising the minimum wage increase inflation and the number of impoverished people? Once you answer the positive and negative questions, take a broader look at the state of the economy, and analyze the long-term effects of raising the minimum wage, you can come to your own conclusions about whether or not it is a good decision. If you conclude that raising the minimum wage would hurt more than it would help, then you can come up with alternative ideas that could help those in need and would not sacrifice the personal security of those who would be negatively affected by the change. This is how creativity works.

The artsy side of creativity is easy as well. If you want to be a writer, then all you need to do is start writing down your thoughts. If you want to write poetry, develop some simple rhymes; after a while they will become more complex as your ability develops. The same technique works with painting, drawing, carpentry, landscaping, and graphic design. Whatever your passion, take the time to work at it. If you have trouble developing your creative side, then study some of the things you enjoy most. If you like movies, for example, learn what goes into the process of producing a feature film, from casting, props, and set designs, to writing scripts. Once you put it all together, you can become more aware of all of these factors the next time you watch a movie. As you become more knowledgeable, you may choose to get involved in one of these tasks on your own, whether it be writing, drawing, or editing your own ideas.

DOING RESEARCH

Access to the Internet means that a wealth of knowledge is right at your fingertips. You can look up anything that you are interested in and will not only find a wealth of information, but also some direction on how to learn or experience more. You can look up information about future professions, disease symptoms, what is healthy to eat, schools you are interested in attending, instructions on how to build or learn just about everything, and much more. Those who are not afraid to research will be more prepared and have better opportunities, because they will be more informed and will have more insight into whatever subject they are tackling. Research can also help you communicate better and make better impressions on those you are trying to connect with; it will show that you are intelligent, that you are truly interested in whatever it is you are pursuing, and that you have the means to find answers and are not afraid to put in extra work to stay ahead of the curve.

ASKING QUESTIONS

You can't learn about something unfamiliar to you if you don't ask. Sometimes it is better to take the risk and ask the question than to pretend you know and then do something wrong. Obviously, if you keep asking the same people questions over and over, they may become frustrated with you and think you don't have any initiative or ability to learn on your own, but if you ask the right questions at the right times, then you'll show people that you are engaged and determined to do the best you can. Knowledge is power, and you can only harness this power by being unafraid to learn all you can. Sometimes you obtain knowledge through coworkers, and sometimes it just takes time and experience, and sometimes you need to do some research.

ENGAGING OPPORTUNITIES

You can't fear opportunities; you have to take advantage of them when they arise. A good percentage of people who succeed had a head start, or someone who helped them get them there. Some of us don't have the same luxuries and have to work harder to climb the ladder. When someone wants to take a chance on you and offers you an opportunity, jump at it. You don't always have to accept what is offered, but it's worth the time to at least listen and learn about the proposal. Acquiring more knowledge should give you a better idea of what is required and what you could gain, and whether or not it sounds like something that is right for you. You can always go back to what you were doing before if the opportunity doesn't work out for you. You'll walk away with new knowledge and the confidence that you aren't scared to try new things. You will never know what you are capable of if you hide behind doubt and fear of failure instead of seizing the moment.

COMPROMISING

Sometimes we feel that our way is better than others. Most of the time it is, at least for us, because it makes sense to us and helps us meet the goals we have set. It is important to understand that other people are trying to meet their goals as well. Compromise means being able to work in a group and finding a solution that gives everyone a chance to win. You may have to give something up, but if you perfect this skill, you should be able to come out on top more often than not. Sometimes you have to compromise because people are simply unwilling to accept change or to go along with a plan that they don't support. This is where compromising is a key skill. If you can find out what they really like about the current plan and what they dislike about the new plan, you may be able to work something out that will show that you have taken all of their concerns to heart and have developed a solution that could benefit them.

The most important thing in compromise is to make sure you don't give up everything just to please the group. If those you negotiate with take everything that is important to you off the negotiating table, then you are no longer working together, and you may need to take a step back and rethink your position.

RELOCATING

You can't be afraid to move around the world if the opportunity presents itself. Experiencing the cultural differences each location offers will bring you a greater understanding of how unique each part of the world is, and you can find subtleties in the way people act. You will have the opportunity to try new foods and flavors. When I moved to California, for instance, I fell in love with Mexican food. I encountered foods I had never heard of before, and many of those foods that I discovered are still some of my favorite dishes. You can get a kick out of hearing how the dialect and slang of a language varies in different regions. Maybe you'll find local activities that are common only to a certain region. Even laws can change from state to state, and it goes without saying that they vary from country to country. If you do plan to move, you should do some research to avoid getting caught unprepared. The quicker you adapt to your new surroundings, the more fun you will have.

ADMITTING YOU DON'T KNOW SOMETHING

This is a huge mistake that I see a lot of people make. Don't be afraid to admit that you don't know something. Some people are scatterbrained, while others can have photogenic memories; most of us are somewhere in between. I admit that I have a horrible memory, but I make good decisions. When I don't know something, I'm the first to ask someone who does. It's always good to be aware of who to go to for what. When you can create a chain of knowledge, you can quickly track down information to fill in any missing holes that you can't answer. People will notice that you're very capable and always prepared. They will see you as an expert and will look to you when they have any issues that they need help with.

Those who try to get by through bluffing or hiding issues will get exposed sooner or later. Their reputations can suffer and they could get fired, put others in challenging situations, and/or lose key friends or contacts. It's acceptable to not know things. If that embarrasses you, then realize that, with a little time and effort, you can spend some time educating yourself and increasing your knowledge base.

TRYING SOMETHING NEW

Those who are afraid to try new things will stay stuck in a rut. The world is vast and complex, and there is a lot to explore and learn if you just open your mind. Those who are adaptable make the best employees and are good friends to have: they are not afraid of being in unfamiliar situations and seem to find their way through any problem. Being adaptable will also enrich you and will place new directions in front of you that you may not have considered before. Don't be afraid to enjoy the things you have, though; it's also good to be committed to the direction in which you are going. (This advice is more for those who feel lost or complacent in life.) Either way, you want to be open to new experiences, since these can help you get closer to your goals.

RELIGION

People practice many different religions around the world. As our society becomes more global, you will become exposed to other faiths and you will find people who are just as devout as you are in their beliefs. Humans have fought wars over religion for thousands of years, and many of these conflicts are still happening today. One religion believes that Jesus Christ is our Lord and savior, while others honor him, but as one prophet among many. Some religions believe in multiple gods and worship a variety of deities.

I have two takes on how you should approach this. First, if religion is a major factor in your life, then don't fear it: spirituality is a beautiful thing. Your devotion shows that you have integrity, loyalty, dedication, and a sense that there is something greater out there than just us. I merely urge that you be cautious not to push your beliefs on others, or you may risk damaging relationships or opportunities. Second, learn from other religions and understand the common messages of peace and love. By learning tolerance, we better learn how to relate to one another and work toward making the world a better place. Religion is a touchy subject. You have every right to be proud of your religion, but in all matters of faith (or lack of faith), you should always extend the same courtesy to others that you would expect from them.

OTHERS' FAILURE

Just because someone has tried to do something and failed doesn't mean that you will fail as well. Since we all develop different skill sets, some of us may be better equipped to handle a situation or task than a friend or relative. In the same way, you shouldn't be afraid to try something because a friend or relative failed, and you're worried that it will cause a backlash of some kind if you succeed. You cannot hold yourself back for fear that others will resent you or that you will suffer the same fate. You can help them by succeeding and then teaching them how to better their odds of doing the same.

KEEPING YOUR COMMITMENTS

Being an honorable person can build good karma both internally and externally. While we all try to get into the best position possible in life, it is important to honor any commitments you've made before making any new ones. This means more than simply associating with one friend over another: it entails taking care of the friends and family members who have helped you along the way, honoring any contracts you have signed, and not going back on your word to people you have made promises to. If people see you as someone who lacks honor who is quick to break promises, then you'll have a hard time finding people who want to hire you, work with you, or work for you. Your personal relationships will also suffer because people will find you untrustworthy and question your motives.

BAD HABITS TO BEWARE OF

The following section lists thirteen bad habits that most of us are guilty of at one time or another in our lives. We need to steer clear of these habits if we want to get ahead in life.

LAZINESS

Laziness is a trained behavior. It is in our nature to find the path of least resistance to gain the largest reward. People who exhibit this trait get by on the backs of others and have learned how to manipulate situations in order to get what they want without having to put in a lot of effort. Maybe their parents spoiled them, maybe they just seem to get lucky all the time, or maybe they have attributes that cause people to want to help them. Whatever the case, laziness will stunt your growth. While of course everyone needs time to relax, those who exert themselves less will ultimately receive less reward. They may be satisfied with merely getting by, but that limits how far they can go toward their goals. Being lazy will cause you to rush through things, to not understand concepts or make connections, and to undervalue important lessons in life. It is hard to build relationships with people who do not contribute the same effort as you: when you work hard toward a partnership, you want to feel like you are getting something back in return. Laziness is not an excuse for ignorance; it is the cause.

DEPRESSION

This is a tough subject. Mental illness is increasingly coming to the forefront. As our society changes and we are losing our personal touch with the world, depression is becoming more and more common. As I mentioned earlier, make sure that if you notice that you don't feel right, talk to a doctor. If you can, try to change your surroundings, alter some of your eating habits, and increase your level of exercise before allowing yourself to be medicated. Mental illnesses such as depression can severely hurt your self-confidence and your desire to put yourself out there; when you do that, you won't accomplish your goals, which will only lead to further depression. You'll think you deserve less than what others deserve and you will settle for relationships that may not reflect your true values and goals. As with most barriers, the only way to get past this one is to find a way to feel positive and motivated: the longer you allow depression to take hold of you, the deeper you will fall into its trap.

OVERCONFIDENCE

Many people think they are so smart and talented that they stop doing the very things that got them where they are. They start taking shortcuts or stop searching for consensus and think that whatever they do is right. This can also cause them to walk over people who may have supported them and who could have continued helping them reach their goals. Again, people who put effort into relationships, even at work, want to know that they are getting something in return. If someone helps you look good, then it is your responsibility to do so in return.

Once you start shutting people out of your life and they no longer feel like you're listening to their ideas, this will hurt you because you will be missing out on opportunities to learn from (and share with) like-minded people. They could very well abandon you in your time of need.

Overconfidence can also cause you to raise your hopes higher than your abilities: when you begin to tackle situations that you can't handle, you can risk your reputation or your career (or both). This could also mean that if you fail, you'll fall harder, only because you expected to succeed. Confidence is a great tool, but be careful to stay grounded, and be aware of how your actions affect those around you.

Dependence

Becoming overly dependent on other people can make it difficult for you to handle things on your own. What will you do if a coworker or classmate you are too dependent on moves to another position or is out sick? If you are too dependent on your parents, you will be in dire straits when they pass on. You need your own inner strength and confidence to accomplish whatever is set before you. We all need help sometimes, and it's wonderful if you have people to lean on, but you also have to be your own person. If you find yourself in a situation where you are so dependent on a parent, friend, partner, or coworker that you aren't doing things for yourself, then you should remove yourself from that situation. People who control everything for you are really trying to gain control over you.

The more dependent you become on someone, the harder it will be for you to let go; that person then has an advantage over you. I have seen relationships where one person controlled all of the finances and had total control over the other person's actions. Without a job or money, that person may stay in a bad relationship in order to survive. This also happens in the workplace, where people feel that they have to stay at jobs they don't like because they are not increasing their skills and fear that their current job is the best they can manage. This is why you have to always push to take on more responsibility, and to learn new things.

Being Overemotional/Complaining

There is a thin line between having passion and being a serial complainer. People with passion work toward a cause they believe in and are willing to risk personal gain for the greater cause, while people who complain are generally unhappy with things that affect them directly; it could be that they didn't get the accolades or compensation they thought they desired. If this is the case, then they really don't have the greater good in mind. If you have a breakdown every time you are faced with a problem, then you will be labeled as someone who is incapable, possibly selfish, and/or the weakest member of the team. When a crisis or better opportunity appears, those who are making the decisions will generally overlook someone whom they conclude is unable to handle pressure or rise to the occasion in favor of someone who is more stable and confident. This doesn't mean that the overlooked person isn't intelligent, doesn't have the ability to improve, or isn't able to do the job well: those who are in charge may simply want to avoid finding out.

Those who spend a lot of time complaining also hurt themselves in the long run. People in power are looking for solutions, and not more problems. If you keep complaining about how this bothers you and how that is wrong but don't do anything positive to lead things in a positive direction, you will appear to be someone who is trying to poison the well and who doesn't care to make actual improvements. I've worked with people who complained every time a change was considered, but they never provided any feedback or alternatives; this not only created tension in the department, but it encouraged other members of the group to adopt this negative behavior. This is how work environments erode from being positive, productive parts of the organization to just the opposite; employees come to work and take less pride in their work, while management may get so tired of hearing complaints that when someone actually does have a legitimate complaint, it may be brushed off. You want to be seen as a problem solver and not a problem creator.

OVERCOMPENSATING

People who do not have their act together often overcompensate: they spend more time doing homework or working later than they need to in order to catch up. Be careful not to stretch yourself too thin, or you will burn yourself out. Don't let people abuse you because you are trying to make a great impression, or because you like to show that you can handle the responsibility. A huge clue to this is that managers overwork the people who prove to be workhorses and then go back and take all the credit. Your effort ends up furthering their careers, instead of your own. Learn how to share the work, trust that other people can do their jobs, or simplify or combine tasks. Do not take on more challenges than you can handle; but if you find that you are, take stock and figure out what you can cut out.

If you are unsuccessful in your profession, then it may be time to look for a different line of work. Don't allow yourself to risk your security over needing to prove you can do something. They say that you can be anything you want, but the fact is that you can *try* to be anything you want. If you aren't athletic enough to be a professional ballplayer, for instance, then aim to be a personal trainer or a sportscaster. If you can't do what your first choice was, then make sure you develop a backup plan. This is part of knowing who you are; sometimes it's best to realize that something is not within your grasp than to torture yourself attempting to do the impossible.

BEING OVERLY CRITICAL

If you are constantly criticizing people, even if you have good intentions, those people will quickly start to dislike you. Some people are overcritical because doing so is the only way they know how to motivate people; the behavior is likely a byproduct of how they were raised. They rationalize that if they make you feel bad, you will work harder so that you will not repeat this mistake. Not everyone thinks or reacts in the same way, however: being tough may motivate some people, but others may become alienated and will interpret your actions as personal attacks. Once people grow to dislike you, it is hard to win them back. Be careful not to be too harsh with people, or you will risk losing them.

ACCEPTING YOUR POSITION

If your choices have left you in a stagnant position, then it is up to you to make the hard decisions you need to make and move on. The only reason you can't enter a new field or land that promotion is because you are holding yourself back. Sometimes you have to go backward in order to go forward, and sometimes you need start over completely. You may need to learn new skills or become better at networking; sometimes it's as simple as letting someone know that you are interested in taking on more responsibilities. If you take no action, however, then you cannot expect any change. Complaining will only make you angrier and will make you feel more hopeless about your situation; this is a good sign that you need to rethink where you are in life, however, and that you need to rethink the best way to get your life back on track.

Taking Opportunities Just for the Sake of Taking Them

Sometimes you find yourself in a job or enrolled in a major at school that doesn't fit you. You wake up one day and realize that you don't get along with the people you are surrounded by, the money isn't enough for the work you do, you aren't getting the right opportunities, or you don't want to be physical therapist after all. Our first reaction is to jump into another role or change classes or to otherwise do something to shake things up.

You need to consider many factors before jumping into a new environment. First, is where you going better than where you are coming from? What happens if you find yourself in a similar position? What if you don't get along with the people in your new setting? Second, can you afford to make this change? Will taking a pay cut affect your ability to pay your bills? If yes, will it only be for a short while? Third, does this change align with your long-term goals? Are you going backward? Will there be more opportunity in the long run? Do you see this change bringing you more satisfaction? Will people perceive you as someone who is quick to give up, or will they identify you as a job hopper who is more concerned with status than contributing to team goals? Are you moving around just because you are easily bored? Finally, will minor changes be enough, or do you need to look at the bigger picture and figure out why you are unhappy at your current level?

If you keep changing your major in college every time you encounter a difficult class, then you may need to seek career advice and to find a program that will better suit your interests. Maybe college isn't for you, and you would be better off getting a certification or going to trade school. Maybe college can't offer you what you are looking for, and you should join the military or the Peace Corps or you should become a small business owner.

I wholeheartedly support learning, growing, and constantly improving yourself, but don't change just for the sake of change. Have a plan, and try to move in steps that will support that plan. Alternately, sometimes we need to change or accept less than what we deserve due to factors that are out of control. Some examples could be working for someone who's making the workplace unbearable, being a part of unexpected layoffs, or learning that your job has been moved to a different state. You may have solid reasons for wanting to make a change, and that is valid. Taking the first opportunity that comes your way may be the only way to salvage your lifestyle. Once you have taken this opportunity and have found stability once again, get yourself back into the mode of looking ahead and planning your future career moves.

SINGLE-MINDEDNESS

There is generally more than one way to accomplish any given task or goal. Your idea, although it may be quite good, may not be the best. Don't be afraid to listen to others' opinions and to see issues from many different angles. Only through probing your idea for weaknesses can you truly find its strengths. In the end, what seemed like a good idea at first might not be as solid as you initially thought, but you can then devise a better solution. If you don't solicit others' views, then you are doing yourself and anyone involved in the task a huge disservice. Those who maintain that they are always right, and that their opinions matter most, will generally alienate their coworkers, friends, fellow students, and even romantic partners. The United States and similarly open countries work best on a system that discourages "group-think" and allows for independent ideas to be brought forth and debated. Having lots of ideas is a great tool, and it is even better to be passionate about those ideas, but sometimes you have to lean on others in order to adjust your ideas so that you may become more successful in life in the long run.

SHOWING WEAKNESS

Sometimes we get ourselves into situations we cannot handle. This happens. The goal is to always be pushing yourself to higher levels of success, but sometimes you'll end up in a difficult situation as a result of that pushing: perhaps by luck, good timing, or the absence of better alternatives, you may be chosen for a job or opportunity that you don't have the skills to accomplish. The best thing to do is to stay calm and start planning an effective way to minimize the damage this could do, not only to your reputation or career, but to your psyche as well.

First, determine what it is about the situation that you are having problems with. Second, if possible, build relationships with those who can help you overcome this situation: if you have someone on your team or a friend who is an expert, then he or she can help steer you in performing some of your responsibilities. Third, do outside research to learn more about the tasks or problems you are faced with. Fourth, talk to your management, teachers, or other people in authority to see if they can help you, either by mentoring you, giving you extra information, or giving you support. Finally, if, after all your efforts, you still feel like success is beyond your grasp, then find an amicable way to depart, and allow those in charge to find someone who may be a better fit. The point is that you don't want to immediately show that you aren't capable without giving it some effort to at least prove to yourself that you did the best you could.

When you overcome adversity, people will recognize that you are capable of great things. Even if you are not a huge success in your current role, the ability to overcome adversity will demonstrate that you have the right tools to tackle tasks that may be outside of your comfort zone.

Not Taking Things Seriously Enough

Taking things too seriously can make you appear rigid and that you don't care about anything. If you often find yourself in stressful situations, however, then mastering the attribute of not taking things too seriously can help immensely in dealing with negative situations without getting bogged down with anxiety. You may accomplish this by joking around or by allowing yourself to minimize the seriousness of any current problems. People will look to you as being a calm and collected person. You shouldn't always display this behavior, however, because if you continually show little interest, or if lacking passion in what you do becomes the norm, then people may come to doubt your loyalty, commitment, or overall interest in your role. You may be passed over for someone whom management feels will have more charisma or other positive qualities.

Gullibility

If others find that they can take advantage of you, then there's a good chance they will. While you want to trust people and hope that everyone has good intentions, this is not always the case. Make sure that you are informed about important events, and do not rely on others to provide you with information. If something doesn't sound right, then do some research, and don't draw conclusions too quickly. People may try to get you to take sides, help to ruin the perception that others have of another person, or use you to get ahead. People who are seen as being foolish will generally be passed over in groups or work settings: they will be seen as low-level contributors, and they will have a hard time dispelling that reputation.

EFFECTIVE TOOLS THAT CAN HAVE NEGATIVE CONSEQUENCES

Every tool you have, whether it appears ethical or not, can be used to personal advantage in most situations. If I am going to encourage you to identify your strengths and weaknesses and to use them to better your opportunities, then I cannot leave out those tools that I may disagree with. If you use these skills for your betterment, avoid getting caught up in the power they can generate. Power is highly corruptive, just as alcohol and drugs are. If you abuse your gifts, you may find success, but you will have trouble making deep and meaningful personal relationships due to the mistrust or dislike these tools can produce.

OFFICE POLITICS

Those who can maneuver around roadblocks by creating effective relationships can prosper from this tool. This includes knowing what battles to fight and which to concede, who to go to for approval, and who to avoid. Some of the ways in which people abuse this tool include backstabbing, brownnosing, or being power-hungry. People use office politics to climb the ladder by pushing others down or by throwing them off the ladder. Backstabbers generally treat people well in public and then do things that cause them to fail, cause others to mistrust them, or make them appear unorganized or out of the loop. Brownnosers will not only betray their coworkers at a moment's notice, but they also spend a lot of time and energy trying to gain favor with those in power.

While networking is important, being overanxious or constantly striving for approval will only prove to management that your loyalty can be bought and sold; they'll believe that whatever you do to others, you may one day do to them. Some managers enjoy the attention, however, and they believe that this type of person can actually help them. People often see power-hungry people as being ruthless; they will do anything to achieve their goals. While it is admirable to have the hunger to succeed, it's a long way to the top, and you need to be careful that you aren't stepping on those who helped you along the way.

People who properly use the office politics tool to their advantage can build strong, powerful relationships and generate a high level of cooperation with their fellow colleagues, while those who abuse the skill will be seen as cold and calculating people who are difficult to work with.

ABILITY TO SELL/PRESSURE OTHERS

Being able to sell things is a great gift. It includes a combination of being charismatic, thinking fast on your feet, having strong communication skills, being knowledgeable about your product, and understanding your customer. Those who have this skill have the potential to make lots of money, they are valuable assets to their organizations, and they are able to turn negative situations into positive ones. One negative side to this skill, however, is that people may feel pressured into buying products they can't afford or don't need. They may be coerced into making decisions too quickly or if given more time to understand the nature of, they may have decided against. They may develop a deep mistrust and/or disdain for your tactics as a result and will avoid any future dealings with you.

People who have this skill generally find that things come easily to them; they may become lazy or have a hard time developing a sense of loyalty as a result. They may also have difficulty saving money, since they always find ways to earn it without much effort. Another issue is that they can get caught up in pyramid schemes or in selling illegal products when they need a quick dollar, rather than taking the time to look for an honest career path that could be just as financially rewarding in the end. They may not think about which opportunities are available to them, or they may not know how to apply for such opportunities. It is also hard to be upset with those who have this gift; in the end, we need to have the self-control to say no if we don't want to buy their services or products.

ABILITY TO MANIPULATE

People who can manipulate situations are generally able to secure the right people, finances, and materials to accomplish the tasks set before them. Sometimes it takes effort to convince people that you know what you are doing, and that the method you want to use is the correct one. Sometimes you need to expose a situation in order to get others to take action. Convincing your boss that you need an extra cashier on the night shift may be difficult, for example, but if you call in sick one night and force the boss to work the register herself, she might change her tune. The art of manipulation is a powerful tool that can help you accomplish great things. Some people use manipulation to pursue their own personal objectives or growth, however, rather than trying to better their groups or organizations. They want something, and they will do everything in their power to get it. If people identify you as a manipulative person, you will have a tough time forging partnerships or getting people to trust you. This is another type of reputation that sticks and is hard to undo.

Forming Alliances
Forming alliances is important in helping you get the proper support while trying to accomplish your goals. Proper use of this tool can lead you to all the right people in all the right places. People who abuse this tool, however, will look to team up with people who may be agreeable or weak, and easy to control. If you appear to prefer being a part of a clique, then people may see you as being uncompromising and hard to work with. If you become too reliant on being a part of a clique, you may find yourself in trouble when those you have aligned yourself with get promoted or leave the group. Once you are labeled with an unpleasant reputation, it may be hard to form new alliances.

Always Being the Go-To Person
Being a go-to person is a great quality: if people go to you when they have a question or need expertise, then your value only increases. Management will see you in a favorable light, and coworkers will look up to you. One negative aspect of this trait is that playing such a role could hurt your ability to move on: management may see you as being too valuable to allow to move up, or they may think that you are not a good management candidate because of your inability to delegate. They may see you as someone who would prefer to remain hands on rather than to allow others to worry about the small details, possibly not doing as good

a job as you would do. Coworkers may think you are a know-it-all or feel intimidated by you. People may also take advantage of you, thinking that if they neglect to do their tasks, you will be there to pick up the slack. Others may take credit for your work because you are too busy being the expert to properly network and accept recognition for your efforts. Or other may be jealous of your efforts and label you a show-off. Again, this is a great skill to have, but make sure you don't let it define you: learn to teach others and do not dominate the group's success. Allow others the freedom to do their job and shine.

BEING TOO QUICK TO ACT

It is wonderful to show that you are engaged and able, that you realize the importance of being an effective member of a team, and that you take deadlines and goals seriously. If you act too quickly, however, you can easily make mistakes or do subpar work. If someone thinks that you're always in a rush and that you do sloppy work, this can affect your ability to advance and be selected to join teams, and people will no longer want to share their goals/tasks with you. Most people work at a moderate pace, and if you are always trying to outdo them, they may have little patience with you. The best thing to do in such situations is to realize that everyone works at different levels, and to be aware of others' speed; as long as they are doing effective work in a reasonable time frame, then you should work closer to their pace. Balance is key. If you are always outworking everyone, but your work is of low caliber, then the advantage of speed may work against you. Quite often, quality is more important than quantity. Working too quickly can also generate stress and can affect you both mentally and physically. This can make you impatient with family and friends and in any other relationships, and it can strain your ability to connect with others on a personal level.

TRYING TO BE EVERYONE'S FRIEND

A charismatic person has many advantages. As a boss, you could potentially have an easier time motivating people. They will be less likely to question your decisions and may even try to emulate your style or mannerisms. People will be drawn to you and will find you interesting, which could help you with networking, building friendships, interviewing for higher positions, and attracting the right type of people. The downside of trying to be everyone's friend is that you set the expectation that anytime there is a conflict, you will give in to the offended party and will try to make that person happy. This can limit your authority or ability to correct bad behaviors in your groups, teams, or departments. The problem may be magnified when people from the same group want different things; trying to please everyone will lead to more turmoil, and, in the end, everyone will blame you for the discord. Sometimes you have to take a stand to make sure that everyone is doing what they are supposed to do.

Others may think that they can take advantage of you because of your close relationship with them. Performing subpar work could become their standard in this case, and they may not take deadlines or goals seriously. In the workplace, they may start to get comfortable with shirking their duties so that they can instead tend to personal matters, such as making phone calls, engaging in online shopping, or working on independent projects that have nothing to do with their job. The same holds true if you're too eager as a friend, partner, or coworker. People will assume you will do anything to make them happy, and they will test the limits. They may give you unpleasant tasks that they don't want to do; some may have you performing all of their responsibilities so that they will be free to pursue personal interests. If you are going to be a good leader, coworker, or friend, it's important to set limits about how you will allow others to treat you. If you want to be a manager, for example, then your employees need to know your expectations, and that failing to meet them can and will result in some form of discipline. Coworkers need to know that you want to be helpful, but that they need to make proper efforts in completing their assigned tasks. And in personal relationships, you need to have enough self-esteem to know the difference between someone needing your assistance and someone taking advantage of you. If it's the latter, be strong and let that person go.

TOOLS

NOW THAT YOU have read about the nine factors to a successful life, completed a SWOT self-analysis, and identified several attributes and abilities to work on or expand, it's time to put your thoughts into action. Below are three tools to assist in motivating you into making some of the changes you desire.

First, I have highlighted a Self-Reflection Tool. This may seem to be an odd tool, but it plays a major role in your mental health. By getting personal with yourself, you can discover unconscious thoughts that may provide insights into your fears, hopes, and dreams. Only by truly understanding yourself and your needs can you make healthy decisions about what it is that you are trying to accomplish in life. Second, the Goal Checklist Tool will aid you in making your goals a reality. You start by listing some of your most important goals, and then you break each one down to see which steps you need to do in order to reach that goal. Understanding why you have chosen the goal, and the obstacles you face in reaching that goal, will better serve you in avoiding failure. Finally, there is the Scheduling Tool. This will be helpful for those who struggle with time management; it shows you how to schedule your time, beginning with your fixed responsibilities. Whatever time remains will be available for you to schedule items such as exercising, taking night classes, engaging in hobbies, or looking for a job. These schedules are merely guidelines that can be modified as needed.

SELF-REFLECTION THROUGH WRITING TOOL

I wrote in chapter 4 about using writing as an effective tool to help self-reflect and analyze where you are in life. If we don't keep in touch with how we are feeling, or we aren't aware of our stressors as we go through life, then we run the risk of harming our mental health, which can lead to anxiety, depression, and anger. As we write, we unearth these windows to our souls. We can peer deep into our subconscious and then determine what bothers us, or we can find things we have locked away and can't (or won't) face. By using this tool, we take a step toward dealing with those issues so that we can be confident, build our mental fortitude, and be prepared to take on new challenges while we strive for our goals.

Writing has always been easy for me. I've always found that the pen moves by itself, and all I have to do when I am done is to go back and figure out what I meant by what I wrote. I also know that others initially struggle with writing. The point of this tool is not to impress others, but to find out what is bothering you, or to explore how you think. You are not limited in how you express yourself through writing: you can do this with poetry, short stories, diary entries, or even random thoughts scribbled down on a pad of paper.

Next, you need to analyze what you write. While this comes easily for me, it may be more difficult for other people. If that is the case with you, then you should have someone whom you trust look over your writing and give you a first impression of what he or she thinks you mean. While this may be difficult to do at first, the more effort you put into refining this tool, the more it will benefit you.

To give you an example of how this tool works for me, I've broken down the lyrics to one of my favorite poems that I've written, called "One with the Sun." I wrote it when I was twenty-two and about to move from Connecticut to California to pursue my dream of being a songwriter. The lyrics are as follows:

One with the Sun
I am blue; shallow is my grave
Insult to jesters of the fool I have made
Without these strings, I am a puppet no more
Who will let me dance, or shall I talk no more?

Cover me with your fire; I could be one with the sun

Calm down, my son; tell me where will you go?
Who will you love and tell me how will I know?
Why always mysterious; will you seize and attest?
Your need for light, invoking greatness

Cover me with your fire; I could be one with the sun
Stare at me with your Aztec eyes; I will wait for the morning to come
I could be one, one with the sun.

These lyrics, at first glance, appear to be gibberish. After reflecting on the time when I wrote it, however, I was able to translate the song in order to give me a picture of where I was at that point in my life and how I was feeling at the time.

The first verse starts with a description of how I felt blue, and that my grave was shallow. This had nothing to do with death; instead, it was more of a reflection of my depression, and how I felt so constricted by life that I felt that I was dying on the inside. The reasons for this outlook were that I was leading a life that made me feel unfulfilled, and the decisions I was making only led me deeper into the hole I was trying to climb out of. I was "insulting fools" with my behavior. I knew I was better than what I was allowing myself to be.

I finally decided to move to California and to pursue my dreams of being a songwriter; that act alone did two things for me. First, I became scared. While I was indeed unhappy at the time, I was also secure. I was taking a huge risk and had no idea what the outcome would be. I didn't know if my choice would lead to an enriching experience, or if it would send me spiraling down even further. Second, and more importantly, I made the decision that I was not a puppet: I had control over my own life, and I couldn't be afraid to try for something better in life. Whether we succeed or fail doesn't really matter: what matters is that we try and that we learn from our experiences. The song then turns into the chorus, "Cover me in your fire; I can be one with the sun." This phrase expresses the notion that you can try to bring me down, but if I keep pushing, I *can* overcome anything. We all have our fears; we all have obstacles, no matter which race, religion, or social class we come from. No one knows what the future holds, but we cannot be captives to fear.

The second verse starts with what sounds like a parent showing concern over a son leaving home. I am close with my mother, so I felt that this was either me envisioning my mother worrying about me, or that I was giving voice to my fears about whether or not I could truly make it. I wondered if I would find love and/or success; most of all, I questioned whether I would live up to my potential and would have the courage to seize the moment if it were cast before me. The second chorus added the phrase, "Stare at me with your Aztec eyes; I will wait for the morning to come." I feel the meaning of this lyric was that the eyes that were looking at me were angry and warlike, and they cast doubt on my aspirations; nevertheless, I would deal with any negative situations, and would endure and move on, undeterred. The eyes also reminded me of a girl I was in love with at the time, and I knew I had to let her go.

Writing this song helped me because I was depressed and I felt like I was failing. I was frightened about taking this chance and going out into the unknown, unsure of what would become of me. This song gave me confidence. Though I accepted my fears, I could no longer be trapped in my current state of being. I had to be brave; I had to make a change. This wasn't gibberish, after all; this was an anthem of my discovering my inner power and my determination to make something more of myself.

If you can search within yourself and extract this kind of emotion and passion, then you will be able to see what may be holding you back from success or causing your anxiety. Only by understanding what is going on inside can you understand, heal, or know yourself better and know in what direction in life you want to move.

GOAL CHECKLIST TOOL

In order to reach your goals in life, you first must know exactly what you want to accomplish, what steps you need to take to progress, what you need to work on to be able to take these steps, what challenges you may face, and what to do if you success eludes you. One way to achieve this is to create a goal checklist where you can list these factors; the checklist can also serve as a guideline for keeping track of your progress and for learning which factors you may still need to work on. If you need help with this list, then ask a friend, colleague, or family member to participate in developing this guide.

In order for this process to be effective, you have to be totally honest with yourself. First, pick goals that are realistic and achievable. If you are deathly afraid of heights, for example, the chances are that you won't be able to become a pilot unless you can overcome that fear. Second, make a commitment to what you have written. Research is an important aspect of your decision-making activities. If you want to get a job as a project manager, for instance, then you need to apply to schools in your area that have a strong program in this field. Having a degree from a school that is preferred by industry leaders will better your chances of attaining an interview. Finally, don't let the amount of work involved or the fact that you may have setbacks deter you from reaching your goal. You cannot succeed if you don't persevere.

To begin your checklist, list your goals on a sheet of paper. They can be simple ones, like learning to play an instrument, or more complicated ones, like becoming an engineer and moving to Cape Canaveral to work for NASA. Don't limit yourself in the initial stages; you really can accomplish anything that you are willing and able to put in the time and effort into.

Example: Goals
Goal one: Get a better job
Goal two: Go back to school
Goal three: Purchase a house

Goal four: Start a family
Goal five: Learn how to ride a motorcycle

Once you have decided what your goals are, then list the factors that can improve your chances of success at those goals. As you list these, you can decide if you are ready and able to take on that goal, or if it'd be better to look into accomplishing some smaller goals first. Some of your goals will be complex, and you may need to take some big steps to reach them. Don't be afraid to challenge yourself, but, again, be realistic. I've used "Goal one: Get a better job" below to illustrate the use of this tool.

To get started, list some reasons behind this goal. Are you unhappy with your career? Do you need more money? Second, outline some steps that you may need to take to accomplish it. What field do you wish to enter? What qualifications do you need to have? Third, set yourself a time frame. Hopefully this will add motivation to the goal and change it from a thought, to a process. Fourth, review some of the attributes above and pick out ones that will help you reach this goal. In this case, being proactive and working on your communication would be key. Fifth, it's important to review what could be some possible setbacks, this way you don't get caught off-guard if or when then happen. Sixth, remind yourself that you need to stay positive and some goals take time to accomplish. Use this portion to encourage and remind yourself that you are on the right track. Seventh, list some things to consider. These are things you can consider if things do not go according to plan. You may need to change your goal or the way you are going about accomplishing it. For finding a job, you may need to get assistance, find ways to network, or begin at an entry level position.

GOAL ONE: GET A BETTER JOB

Current issues:

- You are unhappy in your current career
- You cannot afford your bills

- You want to be challenged
- You don't like the people you work with
- You feel unappreciated

Steps to take:

1. Choose a profession you are interested in
2. Do some research on that profession:
    a. Availability of jobs in your area
    b. Availability of jobs in other areas
    c. Average yearly salaries
    d. Skills/qualifications needed
    e. Testimonies about satisfaction levels in the profession
    f. Advancement opportunities
3. Look for educational programs that can enhance your chances of being selected for an interview
4. Generate a professional résumé
5. Practice answering any questions that you may be asked in an interview

Time frame: Looking to land a job within six months

Attributes that could contribute to meeting this goal: Having patience, being proactive, building skills, having confidence, having the ability to communicate

Possible setbacks:

- You may be competing with stronger candidates
- You may need to start at a lower level than your current position
- You may not be qualified at this time
- Your interview may go poorly
- You may feel the job doesn't sound right for you

Remind yourself:

- Don't give up at the first sign of rejection
- There will be other opportunities
- Achieving your goal may take longer than you anticipated
- You are up against fierce competition
- You need to stay positive

Things to consider:

- If you are unable to reach your goal by the date you've set, you may need to:
  - Revise your goal
  - Check to make sure your research is accurate
  - Seek assistance in reaching your goal:
    - Temp agencies
    - Online job workshops
    - Websites
    - Networking
- Choose more than one possible profession to increase your chances of success
- You may benefit from an internship to get hands-on experience
- Avoid having gaps in your résumé; if you are between jobs, you can either volunteer or return to school to show that you are being active
- When unemployment levels are high, jobs may be scarce

Again, don't be afraid to revise your goal as you go along. You may learn new information, or you may have new experiences that alter your plan. This chart is meant to help guide you and to ensure that you take the right steps to better equip yourself for meeting the challenges that lie ahead.

SCHEDULING TOOL

The Scheduling Tool can help you learn to effectively manage your time. It's easy to get caught up in the daily grind and end up wondering where the time went. This is another factor that causes some people to give up on their goals. They say, "I don't have the time to do that," or "I can't fit this into my schedule." Having a strict regimen isn't always fun, but if your goal is to change your life, this is another step you need to take.

Below I have created a few basic examples of a weekly schedule. Chart A is a representation of the schedule that I followed while I was working full-time and taking college classes at night. Chart B shows a potential schedule for someone who is in school full-time, while working a part-time job at night and on the weekends. Chart C provides a schedule for someone who may have been recently laid off or has been unemployed for a while. You can create a variation of any of these charts that will best suit your lifestyle.

To begin your schedule, make a list of the fixed responsibilities you have in your life. These are tasks that must be done and cannot be changed. This includes going to work, classes, or church. Once you have identified these factors, add them to your chart in order to reserve time for these activities. Don't forget to set aside time for getting ready or driving to each location. Next, create a list of secondary activities that you need to complete each week. They are just as important as the fixed responsibilities, but may allow more flexibility, such as going to the gym, doing household chores, or coaching soccer practice. Once you've filled in the chart with your current responsibilities, you can see what time you have left to pursue your goals. If you want to lose weight, for instance, you can find open slots for exercising. If you want to take night classes, you can match class schedules with your availability. If you're looking for a new job, you can create a set regimen to keep you motivated, and so on. Color coding helps you to quickly identify the different factors and to identify where you have gaps in your schedule.

Let's review the three charts to give you more insight into building your own.

In chart A, I started with filling in my work and class schedules, because these occurred at set times. In order to excel in my classes, I needed to block out enough time for homework and studying. As I discussed in chapter 5, exercise is important for various reasons, so I made sure that I left plenty of time for weekly workouts. I addressed being mentally fit in chapter 4; to help with this aspect, I blocked out some time to sleep in on Saturday and for spending time with friends and family. I also gave myself some time to do whatever I wanted to on Friday and Saturday nights. In chapter 8, I discussed the importance of hobbies. To make room for these, I left some time on Saturday to either play my guitar or to do some yard work, both of which I find relaxing. Finally, I made sure that I had some time for food shopping and doing housework.

In chart B, full-time students will need more time for studying because they are taking a larger course load. They juggle showing up for four to six classes with having enough time for working on projects and studying for exams. Most full-time students also have part-time jobs, which generally take out a huge chunk of their nights and weekends. Some students are also athletes, and they need to practice and travel with their teams. Students require more time for hobbies, exercise, and free time for spending with friends, because they are generally younger and more active than the general population. They may also stay up later than the rest of us, which means that they need more sleep in the morning. Full-time students usually live in dorms or at home with their parents, so time for doing chores and shopping may be lower priorities for them.

Looking over charts A and B, I've considered that most people have differing schedules and that they will place more value on certain factors over others. Sometimes you need more time to do a school project, you may have been asked to work late, there may be a concert you want to go to a concert on a Wednesday night, or other unexpected events may come up. The point of this tool is not to force you to strictly adhere to the schedule (although it will be more effective the closer you come to doing so), but to give you guidelines for fitting in all of the important things in your life. This can be difficult when multiple factors take up a lot of time, such as work, school, friends, family, and a relationship. You may belong to a group or organization such as a music band or a softball team, or you may be a member of a town council. That is another key to this chart: if you cannot fit all of your factors into a week, then you may be taking on too much at once. In that case, you may need to decide what is most important to you right now. If you need the degree to get a better job, for example, then you may need to sit out this softball season and spend less time with your friends. You can't have it all, even if you think you can; the more you try, the more you risk getting burned out, which can seriously affect your ability to accomplish your goals. Losing your job can unravel your ability to fund your lifestyle, for example, and doing poorly in school can make you think that you can't do it, or that it's not worth it. It's difficult to succeed if you don't have the time and energy to give things your all. Sometimes you may find yourself in a place in your life that is difficult to overcome. Perhaps you have been laid off, or you are struggling with mental or physical problems, or you may have ended a relationship and are now on your own. Whatever the reason, give yourself a fighting chance.

Given the still-struggling economy as of this writing, some people face the problem of having too much free time. In chart C, I provide an example of how people who are unemployed might spend their free time to increase their chances of finding a good job. Some important things to consider here are that you need to do things that will help you stay busy in order to maintain your desire and drive to succeed. This is why you want to start every day by either going for a walk or a bike ride or going to a job interview to stimulate yourself. Next, you want to give yourself time to enjoy your hobbies so that your mind is not overwhelmed with the stress of not working or worrying about bills. Doing chores can give you a sense of accomplishment and can simulate the structure of a workplace environment. If you keep yourself healthy and happy, your attitude will stay positive. Make sure to put in plenty of time researching and applying for jobs. You increase your chances of getting hired if you are able to appear confident and knowledgeable about the job you're interviewing for. It's also good to have the chance to talk to as many hiring managers as possible, not only to see if you can find the right opportunity, but also to gain experience and poise in the interview process. You should also plan to spend some time online, networking on sites such as Facebook or LinkedIn.

Your résumé is an important tool in your quest for employment and it's crucial not to have any glaring gaps. Most hiring managers will throw out résumés with chunks of time missing, because they will get the impression that people lack drive or ambition. To combat this, find things to do while you are job hunting. This can be as simple as finding a local organization that you can donate your time to. Going back to college or getting a certification shows that you are serious about making yourself marketable. In chart C, I listed taking online classes instead of going to a physical campus. This helps when you are unemployed, because you can save money on transportation and it leaves you with greater flexibility for scheduling job interviews. And when you do land a job, your class time will not interfere with your new work schedule, because you can learn at your leisure. Some of the pitfalls of unemployment are that you can get used to staying up late and sleeping inconsistently; this can lead to developing bad habits such as always being tired and unmotivated, and it can wreak havoc on your psyche. Combat these bad habits by sticking to a set regimen, exercising regularly, and using blocks of free time to pursue your interests or hobbies. Don't be afraid to get out there and attend functions such as job fairs in order to network and research your career options. Good luck!

Chart A: Work/School Schedule for Returning Students

	Sun	Mon	Tues	Wed	Thurs	Fri	Sat
7:00 a.m.							
8:00 a.m.	Shopping						Sleep in
9:00 a.m.							
10:00 a.m.	Exercise	Work	Work	Work	Work	Work	
11:00 a.m.							
12:00 a.m.							Chores
1:00 p.m.	Hobbies						
2:00 p.m.							
3:00 p.m.							
4:00 p.m.							
5:00 p.m.	Study	Class 1	Exercise	Class 1	Exercise	Exercise	
6:00 p.m.							Free time
7:00 p.m.		Class 2	Study	Class 2	Study	Free time	
8:00 p.m.							
9:00 p.m.							

Free time	Use to unwind/have fun
Exercise	Focus on physical health
Chores	Clean the house/do laundry
Work	Build this schedule around your work hours
Class time	Build time in for your classes
Sleep	Get some extra sleep to stay refreshed
Hobbies	Play video games/music/woodworking (whatever it is you enjoy doing.
Shopping	Groceries/supplies/clothes
Study	Put in the time, and you will do well

Chart B: Work/School Schedule for Full-Time Students

	Sun	Mon	Tues	Wed	Thurs	Fri	Sat
7:00 a.m.	Sleep						Sleep
8:00 a.m.		Sleep	Sleep	Sleep	Sleep	Sleep	
9:00 a.m.							
10:00 a.m.	Work	Class	Class		Class	Hobbies	Work
11:00 a.m.							
12:00 a.m.				Exercise		Chores	
1:00 p.m.		Study	Study		Study		
2:00 p.m.		Exercise	Exercise	Hobbies	Exercise	Shopping	
3:00 p.m.	Study	Hobbies					
4:00 p.m.					Hobbies		
5:00 p.m.		Class	Work	Class		Work	Free time
6:00 p.m.							
7:00 p.m.	Free time				Free time		
8:00 p.m.		Study		Study			
9:00 p.m.			Study			Study	

Free time	Use to unwind/have fun
Exercise	Focus on physical health
Chores	Clean the house/do laundry
Work	Build this schedule around your work hours
Class time	Build time in for your classes
Sleep	Get some extra sleep to stay refreshed
Hobbies	Play video games/music/woodworking (whatever it is you enjoy doing.
Shopping	Groceries/supplies/clothes
Study	Put in the time, and you will do well

Chart C: Schedule When Unemployed

	Sun	Mon	Tues	Wed	Thurs	Fri	Sat
7:00 a.m.							
8:00 a.m.		Exercise	Exercise	Exercise	Exercise	Exercise	
9:00 a.m.							
10:00 a.m.	Volunteering	Online job hunting	Online job hunting	Interviews	Online job hunting	Interviews	Volunteering
11:00 a.m.							
12:00 a.m.							
1:00 p.m.		Shopping	Hobbies		Hobbies	Hobbies	
2:00 p.m.				Free Time			
3:00 p.m.							
4:00 p.m.		Chores	Chores		Chores	Chores	
5:00 p.m.							
6:00 p.m.	Free time	Online networking	Online class	Online networking	Online class	Online class	Free time
7:00 p.m.							
8:00 p.m.							
9:00 p.m.		Free time		Free time			

Free time	Use to unwind/have fun
Exercise	Focus on physical health
Chores	Clean the house/do laundry
Networking	Online networking, making contacts, gathering information
Volunteering	Get involved with a local cause/donate your time
Online class	Take college classes at home
Interviewing	Time spent at job interviews
Job hunting	Time spent looking for jobs
Hobbies	Play video games/music/woodworking (whatever it is you enjoy doing.
Shopping	Groceries/supplies/clothes

ABOUT THE AUTHOR:

Keith J. Pomerleau grew up in Newington, CT, where he began cultivating his creative writing at a young age. In his teens, he sang in bands and wrote lyrics, later learning how to play the guitar. Though he didn't go to college until he was well in his 20's, there he developed the skill of writing long papers. He then began to apply that skill to his creative writings. In 2014 he graduated from Central Connecticut State University with a BS in management. He still lives in CT and currently works for a Fortune 500 company.

The idea to write a book came to Pomerleau in one of his college classes. There, the teacher rekindled Pomerleau's desire to find an outlet for his creativity. After the completion of that class, Pomerleau came up with the idea for two books. The first would be a self-help book (Overcoming Adversity) based on his experiences. It would outline steps to identify and overcome obstacle that stand in place of reaching your goals. The second (Little Green Petal) would be a fiction novel depicting his and his father's relationship.

Though writing a self-help book was not something Pomerleau ever thought he'd do, he realized that he had obtained a lot of useful knowledge that he wished to share to a larger audience than merely his friends and family members.

Pomerleau hopes that these books will be the beginning of more to come. He has already outlined a couple of other fiction novels as well as decided to compile his many years of writing lyrics into a couple volumes of poetry.

35268497R00083

Made in the USA
San Bernardino, CA
19 June 2016